THE
SOUTHAMPTON
BOOK
OF
DAYS

MARY L. SOUTH

First published 2012

The History Press
The Mill, Brimscombe Port
Stroud, Gloucestershire, GL5 2QG
www.thehistorypress.co.uk

British Library Cataloguing in Publication Data.
A catalogue record for this book is available from the British Library.

ISBN 978 0 7524 6534 0

Typesetting and origination by The History Press
Printed in India
Manufacturing managed by Jellyfish Print Solutions Ltd

January 1st

1670: On this day the Corporation distributed its new brass halfpennies and farthings.

The country was bankrupt; there were large amounts of counterfeit money and many traders were producing their own tokens. The traders promised to redeem these with good money, if asked to do so. Southampton traders were doing the same thing and various tokens were circulating in the town. The Corporation felt that, to resolve the situation, a more standard form of local currency should be produced. Having ordered £25 worth of brass 'blanks', these had been stamped with the town's Arms and the inscription: 'The Corporation of Southampton to be distributed to the several shopkeepers, that have occasion for the same, for the benefit of the Poore of the Corporation.' With 480 halfpennies / 960 farthings to £1 (at this time there were 240 pennies to £1), there were a lot of brass coins circulating. Some were still appearing 100 years later, hence the expression 'not worth a brass farthing'. (*See* November 26th) (J.C. Jeaffreson, *The Manuscripts of the Corporations of Southampton and King's Lynn*, 1887, p.31)

JANUARY 2ND

1852: On this day the RMS *Amazon* sailed from Southampton on her maiden voyage to the West Indies and the Gulf of Mexico, with mail and passengers on board. Thirty-six hours later, she was a burnt-out wreck off the Scilly Isles and nearly 100 of the 153 people on board were dead.

The *Amazon* was a wooden ocean-going paddle steamer and it appears that the new large steam engines were overheating; the ship had already stopped several times to let them cool down. At 12.45 a.m., Sunday morning, fire broke out and quickly took hold of the ship, burning so intensely that it was impossible to get close enough for the hoses to be effective. Passengers and crew quickly took to the nine lifeboats, but the new launching tackle was difficult to use and three boats were upset, throwing all their passengers into the water. Other people were reported as burnt or suffocated in their berths. Eventually three boats got away, with varying numbers of survivors on board. The lifeboats drifted in the bad weather and all were eventually picked up, by various ships, with the last survivors arriving at Brest ten days later, before finally returning to England. (*Times* reports from Plymouth and Southampton on 6, 7, 8, 13 January 1852)

January 3rd

1966: On this day, when referring to the demolition of some properties in Laundry Road, the *Southern Daily Echo* inadvertently sparked off controversy about the street's name.

The name had grown up over many years, apparently linked to the fact that many Victorian laundresses had their cottages there. Taking in washing was a perfectly respectable occupation in the Victorian and Edwardian eras, especially for widows with families to support. In the mid-twentieth century, however, some of the residents took offence at the reminder of the road's lowly beginnings and began a petition to change its name, claiming that the name carried a stigma and requesting that it became St Jude's Road. The request was approved for council consideration, but then a counter petition appeared, asking that the name remain unchanged. Some people had signed both petitions! The matter was finally resolved when the council sent out a referendum to all Laundry Road residents, asking if the name should become St Jude's Road. Tradition prevailed; the residents did not want it changed. A month later, the council confirmed that 'the name of Laundry Road be not changed' and so it still remains. (A.G.K. Leonard, *More Stories of Southampton Streets*, Southampton, 1989, pp.110-11)

JANUARY 4TH

1922: On this day it was stated that the bells of Holy Rood had rung in the New Year at midnight on 1 January.

Before Southampton had its civic centre clock tower, it had been the tradition for people to gather outside Holy Rood Church, around the brass cross in the pavement (*see* October 15th), to greet the New Year. Not only was this the municipal church, but the clock had the attraction of the manikin quarter-jacks striking the hour, before the church bells themselves rang in the New Year. Added to the midnight celebrations were the many bells, sirens and whistles of the ships in the docks, and impromptu music with plenty of lusty singing and cheering. Amongst the general cacophony, the sound of the bells had not been heard and the disclaimer was necessary to state that they had rung. The report also said that the Holy Rood tenor bell had celebrated its 600th birthday on New Year's Day, and added, 'age has not dulled the beauty of its tone'. (*Southern Daily Echo*)

JANUARY 5TH

1918: On this day Egbert, the Tank Bank, ended his stay at West Marlands to travel to Swansea for another fundraising session. He had set up camp on the last day of the old year, amidst great celebration, with bands, flags and speeches. Egbert appears to have been the first of several such Tank Banks touring the country, raising money for the war effort.

Publicity for war savings bonds and certificates had begun well before Christmas and people were urged to buy them as Christmas presents. It was advised that they bought them from the Tank Bank, where they would be stamped with a special Tank Bank stamp. The Tank raised £143,000 during its week in the town, with companies competing against one another to raise the greatest amount, and the public benefited from their cut-price sales.

Egbert and his colleagues were damaged British tanks salvaged from the battlefields in Belgium and France. The Southampton one had come direct from the Cambrai Front and behaved impeccably in the town, until trundling down to catch his train on departure, when he unfortunately reversed into a lamppost and knocked it over. Luckily, despite the crowds, no one was hurt. (*Southern Daily Echo*, 31 December 1917 – 5 January 1918)

January 6th

1774: On this day the parish officers told the inoculation committee how many people wanted to be vaccinated.

Inoculation had been known and practised by the more well-to-do members of society for nearly fifty years. It was now becoming the vogue to raise money for the poor to be inoculated – not a completely philanthropic gesture, because it also reduced the danger of passing the disease to the wealthy by contagion. Nationally, it was seen as a means of maintaining the supply of manpower for the workforce and armed forces. Additionally, by proclaiming its commitment to the health of the poor, Southampton was reinforcing its role as a salubrious health resort for its fashionable spa visitors. At this time, smallpox was the most feared of all diseases; victims would be scarred for life, and were often left with debilitating respiratory or arthritic conditions, or even blindness. Inoculation involved placing pus from a smallpox victim's pustules into a scratch on the arm of a healthy person. This gave them a milder attack of the disease and usually lifelong immunity. It pre-dated Jenner's vaccination procedure by seventy years and had been used in China and Asia for hundreds of years already. (Inoculation Book, SCA SC 2/4/1; M. South, 'The Southampton Inoculation Campaigns of the Eighteenth Century', unpublished PhD thesis, University of Winchester, 2010)

JANUARY 7TH

1911: On this day the workhouse guardians discussed the problem of the ambulance horses.

The Board of Guardians met at the workhouse in St Mary's, where one of their concerns was the supply of horses for the ambulance. This came under the jurisdiction of their Farm Committee, who had a contract with Mr Martin to hire two ambulance horses. The contract was due for renewal and the animals would still be needed. Various other stables were willing to undertake the work, so they would obtain quotes from them as well. In the meantime, they would renew Mr Martin's contract for another quarter. The possibility of buying their own horse was discussed, but it was pointed out that they would still need to hire another to work with their horse, as two were needed. Besides, the cost was only £10 a quarter and there were no liabilities for food and stabling. It was decided that overall it would be cheaper to continue to hire, especially when the depreciation of the animal(s) was considered. (*Hampshire Advertiser*, 7 January 1911)

January 8th

1807: On this day Frank Austen, brother of Jane, went skating in Southampton.

There had been a prolonged frost, which had caused the flooded meadows behind the beach to become frozen, forming a rough skating rink. The fact that this area of the town was always prone to flooding (in later years it became renowned for the stench of sewage), and had apparently frozen, indicates that it was very cold indeed. The flood water would have been a mixture of fresh river water from the Itchen and seawater from its tidal estuary. This salty mixture would have needed a temperature lower than zero in order to freeze.

Earlier, Frank and Jane had visited Mrs Lance at her home in Bitterne, which was 'a handsome building in a very beautiful situation'. Jane observed, however, that the Lances '... live in a handsome style and are rich and she [Mrs Lance] seemed to like to be rich, and we gave her to understand that we are far from being so; she will soon feel therefore that we are not worth her acquaintance'. (D. Le Faye, *Jane Austen's Letters*, Letter 49, Oxford, 1997)

JANUARY 9TH

1607: On this day William Shishe of Winchester came to the Assembly to have his son's apprenticeship cancelled.

Shishe complained against Robert Hollyehocke, a basket maker of Southampton, for making 'hard measure of dealings and evill usage … towards Wiliam Shishe his apprentice, son of William Shishe the father [who] having given unto Hollyehocke forty shillings (£2) in money with his son at the [beginning] of his apprenticehood, [he had] not served above two years by reason of his said master's hard using of him'. (J. Horrocks, *Assembly Books of Southampton, Vol. I, 1602-1608*, Southampton, 1917, p.46)

———•◆•———

1997: On this day it was reported that six of the seven dwarfs appearing in the pantomime *Snow White and the Seven Dwarfs*, in Southampton, were suffering from influenza. The only one unaffected was 'Sneezy'! (*Southern Daily Echo*, 9 January 1997)

JANUARY 10TH

1921: On this day two cases of unmuzzled dogs were brought to court and the owners fined.

A muzzling order had been brought into effect due to the presence of rabies in the area. A dog with the disease, from Sholing, had been found at Winchester. This was the first recorded case, but then a case had been found at Bishopstoke, where a pony had caught the disease. Muzzling dogs has always been the first and probably the best line of defence against the spread of rabies into the human population. The order stayed in force throughout the year. The local newspaper correspondence column carried the subject for several weeks, with complaints from dog owners and concerns from others. Then, as now, it is the high fatality rate of the disease, accompanied by its alarming symptoms, which frightens people. The best-known symptoms are the excessive saliva produced by the victims (the virus concentrates in the salivary glands), a fear of water, and irrational, excitable behaviour. It is the combination of excitability and excessive saliva which makes the potential bite from a 'mad dog' dangerous. The UK was considered rabies-free from the beginning of the twentieth century, so this is an unusual report from Southampton. (*Southern Daily Echo*, 10 January 1921, and subsequent published correspondence)

JANUARY 11TH

1997: On this day a couple revived their pet goldfish with the kiss of life.

When Mr and Mrs Day's garden pond froze solid overnight, during the sub-zero temperatures, they were horrified to see their two large goldfish trapped within the block of ice the following morning. Carefully chipping away the ice around the fish, they brought their two lifeless pets indoors to remove the final ice fragments. Taking one fish each, they began to massage the tiny, fishy hearts and blow air into their mouths. To the Days' delight, their efforts were rewarded and both fish revived. To help them on their way, Mrs Day made a bowl of cold, weak herbal tea which the fish swam in to complete their cure. Needless to say, they were not returned to the pond outside until the weather had improved and there was no danger of the pond freezing again. (*Southern Daily Echo*, 11 January 1997)

January 12th

1854: On this day, Philip Klitz died at 24 Portland Place in Southampton.

He was a member of a large and musically gifted family, being a talented pianist, organist, violinist and composer himself. The family business was centred on music, with members repairing, tuning, playing and selling pianos. Their first shop was established in Lymington, by Philip's father, at the end of the eighteenth century. Philip came to Southampton in 1829, as a Professor of Music – teaching, performing and composing for the piano and violin. He gained the highest accolade for theoretical musicians by election to the Contrapuntists' Society, after composing the necessary four-part fugue. At some period, he was also the Provincial Grand Organist of Hampshire for the Masons. He did not, however, limit himself to classical-style music, and composed popular dance music and ballads as well. Also a conductor of distinction, Philip conducted the great violinist Paganini when he appeared at Southampton on 30 August 1832. At the opposite end of performance expertise, Philip also conducted his five-year-old son when he performed in public, with his concertina, to the delight of the audience in the Victoria Rooms. (Friends of Southampton Old Cemetery Newsletter, November 2008)

January 13th

1609: On this day Richard Jennings' wife was brought to court for entertaining unruly people in her house.

She ran a tippling house in East Street and had already been in trouble, at the previous court, for having rogues and wandering persons in her home. The Corporation was concerned about strangers or newcomers staying in the town for two reasons: either they might become a drain on the town's finances if they became sick, or they might become a source of competition for the town's own tradesmen. The local burgesses paid for the privilege to trade, and expected those privileges to be upheld and protected by the Corporation. Mrs Jennings had also committed the crime of having a charmaid in her house. The officials were especially hard on charmaids and, rightly or wrongly, equated them with prostitutes. However, this woman was claimed to be Mrs Jennings' sister and employed as a servant. She promised to go into service elsewhere. It is not clear if this was at another establishment in Southampton, or another town. Did Mrs Jennings regard this as an unlucky Friday 13th appearance at court? (J. Horrocks, *Assembly Books of Southampton, Vol. II, 1609-1610*, Southampton, 1920, p.2)

JANUARY 14TH

1911: On this day, 'one hundred happy lads from the Southampton Gordon Boys' Brigade sat down to a sumptuous repast'. This was the Brigade's annual dinner, held at its headquarters in Ogle Road, and had been provided by friends and subscribers of the Brigade; some of these now waited on the boys.

The Gordon Boys' Brigade had been set up as a memorial to General Gordon, after his death at Khartoum in 1885. It gave employment to poor boys by providing messenger, household and gardening services across the town. The boys were provided with a blue serge uniform and a pillbox hat, becoming a familiar sight running through the streets. They were obliged to report for parade drill every morning, but in return each was allowed to keep three quarters of the fee paid for his services. In addition, the Brigade ran a savings bank for them. Originally set up in the High Street, the Brigade outgrew these premises and transferred to new headquarters in Ogle Road (*see* August 10th). Other Gordon Boys' Brigades were set up in towns and cities to commemorate Gordon, but only Southampton could boast that this particular branch was in the town of his family home. (*Hampshire Advertiser*, 14 January 1911; M. Taylor, *Southampton: Gateway to the British Empire*, London, 2007)

JANUARY 15TH

1997: On this day, baby giraffe Matilda was born at the local wildlife park and, following the park's tradition for naming baby female giraffes, she was given a royal name.

Her mother, Dribbles, was not royally named, but at twenty-nine she was the oldest breeding giraffe in the country. Twenty years earlier she had been involved with the sad story of Victor, the giraffe who did the splits. The popular story of the time was that Victor had slipped whilst mating with Dribbles. Poor Victor was down on the ground with his hind legs splayed out each side, unable to get up. The story hit the press and became international news, with daily reports on his condition and attempts to raise him. The biggest danger was the change of blood pressure to either his brain or heart if he was lifted mechanically. Eventually, this was the only option. A special sling was made and a crane was brought alongside his enclosure. The attempt was made, but the feared heart attack happened and Victor collapsed and died. Some months later, Dribbles gave birth to a baby female giraffe. Only one name was possible – Victoria; the royal name tradition had begun. (*Southern Daily Echo*, 15 January 1997)

January 16th

1841: On this day, trains on the London & South Western Railway were delayed up to ten hours due to a heavy drift of snow between Andover and Basingstoke. Others in the New Forest were delayed due to floods. (*Hampshire Telegraph & Sussex Chronicle*, 18 January 1841)

———◆———

1912: On this day the local newspaper produced two headlines next to one another, giving the reader an unfortunate impression.

The first headline, 'Butcher Mangled by a Train', was immediately followed by another headline, reading, 'Southampton Butchers Banquet at South Western Hotel'. The first story was the sad tale of a depressed unemployed butcher, who had left to see his brother off at the railway station. His body was found later on the track. The jollier second story was about the local butchers and their enthusiasm for the Southampton cattle market. They wanted to have a large Christmas show and market, as well as the regular cattle markets. It was felt that this was currently lacking and they wished to rectify the omission. (*Southern Daily Echo*, 16 January 1912)

January 17th

1433: On this day the Corporation held a feast for themselves in the Guildhall, above the Bargate.

The amount of food consumed and the necessary preparations make interesting reading. The list of food included bread, beef, five pigs, thirty-two chickens, twenty rabbits, eleven suckling pigs, eighty eggs, cheese, dates, raisins, currants and large grapes. This was washed down with seven flasks of wine, a half-gallon (2.2 litres) of sweet wine and thirty gallons (134 litres) of beer. Since meat was not always fresh, spices were needed to make it palatable; the list therefore also included 1lb of pepper, large amounts of salt and vinegar, and other spices like mace and saffron. Bizarrely, two ovens were built in the hall to do the cooking on the spot. To add to the cost of the meal, the ovens needed fuel, tin cups and plates were either bought or hired, fresh rushes were spread on the floor, and cooks and minstrels were hired. Oddly, all the provisions were provided and collected from the Isle of Wight. The total cost for everything, including transport from IOW, came to approximately £2.50. (H. Gidden, *Stewards' Books of Southampton, Vol. I, 1428-1434*, Southampton, 1935, pp.47-9)

1841: On this day, Elizabeth Pearce died in squalor in Castle Court. Her body, when found, was covered in vermin. (*Hampshire Telegraph & Sussex Chronicle*, 18 January 1841)

JANUARY 18TH

1862: On this day the American Civil War came to Southampton.

In November, the Federal warship, the *James Adger*, had put into Southampton for repairs and provisioning. Britain was neutral during the American Civil War, so this was acceptable. Meanwhile, the Confederate ship, the *Nashville*, was crossing the Atlantic. On the way, however, she attacked a Federal merchant ship, the *Harvey Birch*, in the Channel. Knowing that this would be seen as piracy if the ship was taken, the *Nashville* took the crew off and then burnt the merchantman. Needing repairs and provisions itself, the *Nashville* also docked in Southampton, and released the *Harvey Birch*'s crew ashore, resulting in fighting between the two sets of onshore crews. The Federal government regarded the attack on the *Harvey Birch* as an act of war and sent the warship, USS *Tuscarora*, to prevent the *Nashville* leaving Southampton. *Tuscarora* blockaded the mouth of the River Itchen on 18 January. Now Southampton had three American warships in its waters. The *James Adger* was in no danger from the *Tuscarora*, but the *Nashville* needed to be separated. The British government decreed there should be a twenty-four-hour delay between the departure of the two ships, to be enforced by the Royal Navy. Eventually, on 4 February, *Nashville* sailed from Southampton while *Tuscarora* was forced to wait another twenty-four hours to give chase – unsuccessfully. (M. Hughes, *Stand-off in the Solent: The American Civil War Comes to Hampshire*, Winchester, 2002)

JANUARY 19TH

1838: On this day it was decided to sink an artesian well on the Common.

The town was growing so fast that the supply from the three reservoirs already on the Common would soon be inadequate. London engineer, Thomas Clark, had given a favourable report after experimental borings during the previous two years. A contract was signed in March 1838 – not with Clark, but a local plumber, Collyer. After a year, he backed out and four partners took over. In 1842 they had reached 560ft and no water; at 1,260ft a trickle had been achieved, but the partners surrendered their contract in 1845. Afterwards some boring went on from time to time, until 1883 when a depth of 1,317ft was reached and very little water was produced. Two years later, the plans for the Otterbourne waterworks were approved and the need to provide the town with water from its own resources became obsolete. The well was capped with a large stone cover and the project was abandoned. The cover can still be seen a short distance north-east of the boating lake, on the Common. (*Southampton Common*, Southampton, 1979, p.18); (A. Patterson, *A Selection from the Southampton Corporation Journals 1815-35, and Borough Council Minutes, 1835-47*, Southampton, 1965, p.91)

January 20th

1940: On this day, rodents made the headlines.

It had been discovered that one rat had managed to support two families comfortably on a local poultry farm. When the nests were discovered, a food store of twenty dead chickens was also uncovered. Local people were encouraged to set up rat clubs to destroy the pests. There was already a scheme at Botley which paid one penny for every rat tail brought in. The Hampshire Agricultural Committee had set up a grey squirrel competition and would pay £25 prize money for the largest number of grey squirrels killed between this day and 30 April 1940. A bounty of 3*d* per tail would be paid to everyone bringing these to the Committee. (*Hampshire Advertiser & Southampton Times*, 20 January 1940)

JANUARY 21ST

1758: On this day a farmer at Millbrook took pity on a destitute soldier.

He found the man dressed in a blue coat, red waistcoat and red plush breeches but lying on the ground. His clothes were in a ragged condition and he was very weak. The farmer got the man into his waggon and took him home, fed him and gave him drink. However, the man was so full of lice and other vermin that the farmer did not want him in the house, but instead made him a bed in the waggon inside the barn. Sadly the man died, which is when it was discovered that he had an Ensign's commission in his pocket for a regiment at Plymouth, but no money. It is likely that he was one of the sick and wounded soldiers regularly billeted in Southampton during the eighteenth century. The hospitals were only temporary affairs and men were discharged as soon as possible. This is a sad little story underlining the poor state of much of the military at this time, but also shows how people were willing to help complete strangers, if they could. (*London Gazette*, 21 January 1758; M. South, 'The Southampton Inoculation Campaigns of the Eighteenth Century', unpublished PhD thesis, University of Winchester, 2010, p.26)

January 22nd

1900: On this day the first electric tram service, from Shirley, was inaugurated amidst great celebrations.

The Tramways Co., using horse-drawn trams, had been bought by the Corporation eighteen months earlier. New tracks were laid and the overhead electric lines installed, using electricity generated from the Electric Light & Power Co., in preparation for the electrification of the trams. This did, however, bring the Bargate problem to a head. The trams needed to go either through or round the building, which was still the main access point to the High Street and was completely surrounded by other buildings. Various solutions were suggested, including selling it to America – which prompted a general outcry, including this rhyme from *Punch*:

> What's this I hear? Southampton Bar
> Is doomed to desecration?
> Echo it near and wide and far,
> Arouse the English Nation!
> Shall omnibus assert a right,
> Or penny Tramway Car?
> Up! Up! Ye holders of the right,
> Defend Southampton Bar!

The protests gave the Corporation second thoughts and, instead, special trams were designed to pass through the existing gateway. (A. Rance, *Southampton: An Illustrated History*, Southampton, 1980, p.128)

JANUARY 23RD

1913: On this day Alfred Capper would return to his hometown to give a demonstration of thought transmission and other mysterious phenomena. The performance would take place during the evening at the Hartley Hall, and again on Wednesday, 29 January, at the Royal Victoria Rooms.

Capper was said to have travelled over 50,000 miles before finally returning home. His performances had been acclaimed in every quarter of the globe and he had given demonstrations to every crowned head in Europe. As well as these activities, he had published a parody on Robert Southey's poem, 'The Battle of Blenheim'. A long extract from Capper's lampoon was printed in the newspaper, as an encouragement to readers to either attend Capper's performances or buy the publication. Its satire has not worn well for the modern reader and would probably do little to recommend Capper to an audience nowadays! (*Hampshire Advertiser*, 18 January 1913)

JANUARY 24TH

1921: On this day the problem of discharged oil in Southampton Water was complained about by Lord Montague of Beaulieu. His Lordship reported seeing only six swans alive at Millbrook, where there used to be 200 or 300. The birds were staying on land trying to clean their feathers, and dying on the shore.

Shipping was ignoring the 3-mile rule for discharging waste oil into the sea – not only did this have disastrous results for the swans, it was also likely to contaminate local fisheries and local fish, so affecting people's livelihoods and posing a threat to health. The yachting fraternity had already complained about the discolouration to their vessels, the unpleasantness of the water itself and the foul smell. Waterside homes voiced the same concerns and problems. Philip Curry of the Harbour Board proposed increasing the fine to ships to a maximum of £5, but said it was difficult to catch the culprits. Nothing changes! (*Southern Daily Echo*, 24 January 1921)

January 25th

1950: On this day, in the grounds of Blighmont Nursing home at Millbrook, Marcus, a baby piglet, was born. He was discovered to have a leg injury, whereupon Sister Jones and the other nursing staff took charge and whisked him off for specialist nursing. He is reported to have being doing well and, from the picture, thoroughly enjoyed all the female attention. (*Southern Daily Echo*, 31 January 1950)

1950: On this day two cheques for $100 were presented to the Revd G. Hales of St Mary's as a donation towards the rebuilding and refurbishment of the church. One of the cheques came from the New York State Maritime College and the other came from the college alumni. There were strong links between St Mary's and the American college; its first training ship, the USS *St Mary*, had visited Southampton at the beginning of the century and the 'Bells of St Mary's' was the college song. (*Southern Daily Echo*, 25 January 1950)

JANUARY 26TH

1950: On this day a boy was marooned on the island in the middle of Cemetery Lake, on the Common. This was the second such occurrence in two years, with the same results as the first time.

Rescue was delayed because there was no boat available. The police had to send to the Lido (swimming pool) for a suitable craft to rescue the boy. Before the dinghy could be used to reach the island, it was necessary to break the ice on the lake! The ice was treacherously thin in places; nonetheless, the icy stories continued over the next couple of days, with skaters ignoring the warning notices and thoroughly enjoying the frozen lakes. The same could not be said for the swans, and the ice was broken to provide them with some access to open water. (*Southern Daily Echo*, 26 January 1950)

January 27th

1778: On this day, John Bullar was born at his parents' home in the High Street, the first of their eleven children.

After being educated at King Edward VI Grammar School, John Bullar became a schoolmaster in the schools he set up in Bugle Street, Moira Place and Prospect Place. He was a member of the Above Bar nonconformist church and a great champion of liberal causes, being a prominent campaigner against slavery. Later in his life he became deeply involved with the newly established Hartley Institute and helped to shape its early direction before it became the university of today. Whilst he pursued his own concerns for matters affecting the town – including the production of geographical and historical guides for tourists – he was also encouraging his two doctor sons, Joseph and William, in their efforts setting up the Royal South Hants Hospital. No wonder the town boasts a Bullar Road, remembering two generations of the same family who helped shape Southampton during the nineteenth century. (Dictionary of National Biography online)

JANUARY 28TH

1999: On this day, council officials admitted they were wrong in claiming that two large horse chestnut trees were damaging the city's Cenotaph. They had thought that the roots of the trees were undermining the memorial.

The horse chestnut trees in the parks are a well-known feature of the city and, when plans to fell the two nearest to the Cenotaph became known, protesters made their voices heard. During spring 1998, protesters occupied the two sixty-five-year-old trees to prevent them being felled. Further discussions between both sides led to an agreement that the council would call in independent experts, to carry out a full assessment of the trees. And the eco-warriors came down from their perches. Eventually, evidence came to light that the fears about potential damage were probably ill-founded. The arboriculturalists' report concluded that there had been no damage to the Cenotaph in the past, and that it was 'highly unlikely' the trees would cause any in the future. It was predicted that, as these were healthy trees, they could live up to 150 years of age. (*Southern Daily Echo*, 28 January 1999)

JANUARY 29TH

1924: On this day a discussion on the buildings called 'follies' was published, reasoning that a public building which had cost a large amount of money had to be called a folly. However, there was another folly which had been in the town for a while: '… a house, which owing to some curious mistake, contained no doors and was the cause of much amusement at one time, although the necessary doors had since been added.'

1924: On this day the Southampton Radio Society received a lecture about the latest developments in amplification, using two valves. These produced two stages of high frequency and two stages of low frequency; crystal rectification produced volume for the human voice that could be heard 200 yards away, with very little distortion. (*Southern Daily Echo*, 29 January 1924)

JANUARY 30TH

1889: On this day a gymnastics competition between Southampton and Bournemouth was held at the Drill Hall of the 2nd Volunteer Regiment in Carlton Place. This was the first round in a competition organised by the National Physical Recreation Society.

Each team had eight members, competing in: hand-over-hand rope climbing (without using feet), with points awarded for the height climbed; running high jump, starting at 4ft 4in (1.3m), with points won for every extra inch; a voluntary exercise on the rings (steady or swinging), which excluded somersaults and was marked according to strength, skill, agility and grace; and, lastly, a ten-minute combined display of dumb-bell exercises from each team.

In the dumb-bell display, the Bournemouth team caused some surprise by performing to music played on the piano 'with which they kept remarkably good time'. Their graceful movements 'seemed to find greater favour with the judges than the more muscular ones of the Southamptonians', said the report. It is clear that the reporter favoured the Southampton team (which did win overall) and its 'muscular' approach, but the Bournemouth team's use of musical accompaniment gave a foretaste of what we have come to expect as normal from gymnastic displays. (*Hampshire Advertiser*, 10 February 1889)

January 31st

1816: On this day Charles Ward was killed while rescuing children from a fire in St Michael's parish.

The fire had started in the house of a straw-bonnet maker at 11.30 p.m., quickly engulfing the building. Fire bells and the bugles of the militia were sounded. Two engines, the South Hants Militia, and about 200 people arrived. There were problems with faulty pipes and a water supply was not available. By midnight the fire had spread to the adjoining house, where ten people, including six children, were sleeping. They were roused when the front door was broken down and they heard cries of 'Fire!'. The children were in the upstairs room, which was already alight. Ward forced his way upstairs twice to bring children down to safety. He, and others, then tried to save some of the property in the burning houses, but the front of the building collapsed and killed him. A water supply had still not been found; eventually, one came from a tallow chandler's house. At 4 a.m. the fire was out, after four houses and a stable had been lost. Two men who leased the building were taken into custody when it was discovered they had insured it for £1,000 just two days previously. Ward was buried with military honours at Nursling on 6 February. (*Hampshire Telegraph & Sussex Chronicle*, 9 February 1816; *Hampshire Chronicle*, 9 February 1816; plaque in St Michael's Church)

FEBRUARY 1ST

1921: On this day it was advertised that Mr Joe Hastings had taken over the management of the exhibition and Fun City at Shirley Rink.

> There had been a complete transformation and the entertainment was undoubtedly catching the public imagination, because crowds were flocking there every day and some evenings there were many that had to be turned away. The secret of its success was its appeal to young and old alike; the attractions included a grand circus; free dancing; lucky dip; an old English fair and every Thursday a fancy dress dance was held.

Mr Hastings was not intending to stay long but it was advertised on 21 February that he would be extending his activities until 21 March. During the First World War the Shirley Rink had housed prisoners of war, so Mr Hastings' efforts were a welcome return to normality. (*Southern Daily Echo*, 1 February 1921)

———•———

On this day it was also reported that willow trees were in leaf, well in advance of the normal season. It had been a very mild winter, with spring flowers appearing in January and even strawberry plants producing green fruit in local gardens, where, unfortunately, there was not enough warmth for them to ripen. (Southampton Pictorial Annual)

FEBRUARY 2ND

1553: On this day, John (Bilious) Bale was consecrated as Bishop of Ossory, in Ireland. He was an enthusiastic supporter of the Protestant Church, often making controversial comments, and had been described as 'an angry wasp stinging all', hence his nickname of 'Bilious'.

Bale had been Rector at Bishopstoke, near Southampton, since 1551, and during that time had been seriously ill, possibly suffering from the influenza known as the 'Great Sweat'. King Edward VI admired Bale's religious views, but believed that Bale had died during his sickness. When Bale heard this, he travelled to meet the King at Southampton during Edward VI's visit to the town (*see* August 14th). The young King was overjoyed to see Bale fully recovered, and appointed him to the vacant see of Ossory. When Mary Tudor reinstated Catholicism, Bale went into hiding, and tried to reach the Netherlands. On arrival in Dover, to cross the Channel, he was arrested and held in gaol for several weeks. At the end of this time he said that he was 'so full of lice as I could swarm', but nonetheless managed to make a payment of £30 to reach Holland. (Dictionary of National Biography online)

FEBRUARY 3RD

1779: On this day it was reported that a lobster smack sailing between Southampton and Guernsey had been taken by a French privateer, seven leagues off Portland.

At this time, there was so much piracy and privateering taking place that local and national newspapers published lists of privateer actions, including British retaliatory efforts. The reports recorded the cargo, the names of the vessels involved, and often included where the prize (captured ship) was taken and/or what happened to it ultimately. On this occasion, the event was considered so insignificant that no mention of the vessels' names were included in the report – perhaps the catch of lobster and the nationality of the privateers merely reflects a yearning for gourmet food by the French crew! (*Public Advertiser*, 8 February 1779)

FEBRUARY 4TH

1684: On this day, both the rivers of Southampton were frozen right across. On the River Test, or Anton, it was possible to travel from Marchwood to Millbrook. Thomas Marteine made this journey, in his horse and cart, while many others were travelling across the ice on the frozen River Itchen, in both directions. The frost is recorded as having started before Christmas and continued well into February.

During the medieval and Tudor periods, the rivers were not so well dug out or embanked as in later times. This meant that the rivers were shallower, slower moving and more prone to flood across the low-lying land on either side. In this situation, they were more likely to freeze when the conditions were right and, in the Great Frost of 1684, conditions, in what has been called 'the Little Ice Age', were exactly right. Large areas of flooded, low-lying land froze from the Thames and along the south coast. (J.S. Davies, *A History of Southampton*, Southampton, 1883, p.365)

FEBRUARY 5TH

1631: On this day William Barkeseale was accused of witchcraft.

William Nutley said that Barkeseale had been involved with a plot to loot a ship in the harbour by casting the crew into a deep sleep before the thieves went on board. Moreover, Barkeseale was believed to have the ability to foretell where lost or stolen goods could be found. Nutley had wished him to find some linen cloth that had been stolen from him at the Bear Inn. Barkeseale said that anyone trying to find stolen goods had to undergo three days of prayer and fasting beforehand, in order to raise a spirit, but even then the only person capable of seeing the spirit would be a 'true maid' of about eleven or twelve years of age. Evidence was produced that Nutley's maidservant had been sent to Barkeseale and that she had returned with four names for the supposed robbers. The wizard charged 40s for his services, but did promise that this would be returned if the linen was not recovered. (R. Anderson, *Examinations and Depositions 1622-1644, Vol. II*, Southampton, 1931, pp.104-9)

FEBRUARY 6TH

1795: On this day a widow was indicted for receiving sheets and blankets which had been stolen from the army stores in the locked warehouses. The memorandum, in St Michael's parish register, comments that this was the same day her husband was buried. Only John Gould, aged forty-five, was recorded as a burial that day, so presumably this was his widow.

The bedding had been left behind when the army left the town in August, and it was locked in the warehouses. The troops had been brought to the town by transport ships – sick and dying from typhus fever – in January the previous year. Temporary hospitals were set up in warehouses around the town for them. These included the Sugar House in Holy Rood parish. Typhus spread into the town, causing the deaths of many townspeople, and did not lessen until late autumn. When the winter became one of the hardest on record, with average temperatures of -1°, the temptation of the stored blankets became too great. The warehouses were broken into and the infected bedding sold to the people. In March the death rate was frightening as the sickness spread again. (M. South, 'Epidemic Diseases, Soldiers and Prisoners of War in Southampton 1550-1800', *Proceedings of the Hampshire Field Club and Archaeological Society, Vol. 43*, 1987, pp.185-96)

FEBRUARY 7TH

1902: On this day the annual tea party and 'Christmas Tree' had just taken place at the Wesleyan schoolroom in East Street.

Three-hundred-and-fifty children had received tea, buns, oranges, toys and articles of clothing. All the gifts had been provided by donations, together with money collected by the Band of Hope in East Street. The Committee wished to thank everyone for their donations, which had 'brought gladness to many a young heart'. The choice of gifts for children invariably seemed to include clothing, which probably underlines the poverty prevalent in the town at this time.

———— • ◆ • ————

Another news report in the same paper underlines the hazards of working life. A seventeen-year-old railway worker, from Pear Tree Green, had been crushed to death between the carriage buffers of a passenger train in Southampton Docks station. He was a porter and appeared to have been crossing from one platform to another when he became trapped. He had been on night duty and his body was not discovered until the morning. (*Southern Daily Echo*)

FEBRUARY 8TH

1911: On this day it was reported that Mrs Pankhurst had spoken at the Palace Theatre in Southampton.

The theatre stage had been decorated with banners in green, white and violet, the adopted Suffragette colours. Each colour had its own symbolic meaning: purple represented the 'royal blood that flowed in the veins of every Suffragette', white demonstrated purity of life, while green stood for hope and new beginnings. Slogans on the banners displayed messages such as: 'Who would be free themselves must strike the blow' and 'Through thick and thin when we begin'. Mrs Pankhurst was described as a quiet little figure in black, who outlined the case for women's enfranchisement quietly and moderately. However, she pointed out that 'because women of the twentieth century had been driven to extremities by continual refusal, their claim was seen as extreme, whereas it was very moderate … women had no desire to be like men, they appreciated the differences … but there was a woman's point of view on every issue … and a degree of militancy was justified to bring their cause to the forefront'. After an enthusiastic response from the audience, Mrs Pankhurst answered questions and left for a private tea party. (P. Johnston, 'Suffragettes, Suffragists and Party Politics in Southampton 1904-14', *Proceedings of the Hampshire Field Club, Vol. 39*, 1983, pp.201-11)

FEBRUARY 9TH

1774: On this day the first campaign to inoculate the poor against smallpox ended.

Two-hundred-and-forty-one poor people had chosen to be treated by the town surgeons to protect them against the disease. As well as the obvious health advantages, vaccination also gave employment benefits. Potential employers often specified a preference for inoculated servants in their advertisements. Not only did employing such people reduce the danger of the infection being brought into the house, it also provided an immune servant who could safely nurse anyone who later fell victim to the disease. In 1774 smallpox was nationally widespread and Southampton was concerned that its reputation as a health resort might be damaged. The free protection of the poor was quickly used to advertise the safety and healthiness of the Southampton environment. (Southampton Inoculation Book, SC2/4/1)

FEBRUARY 10TH

1297: On this day Sister Elena, one of the sisterhood of God's House, started her vow to eat 'nothing that had suffered death' until Easter, 14 April. She was not going to eat meat for the next nine weeks, but rely on vegetables. She was paid one farthing a day for each day, being 16*d* (7p) altogether.

Sister Elena could have been following the lead of Sister Joan, who appears to have been a committed vegetarian and did not 'eat flesh throughout the year'. It's likely that fish did not count as 'flesh' and that she used some of her daily farthing allowance to purchase fish. Altogether she was paid 7*s* 7*d* (38p) per year for her subsistence. Obviously vegetarianism was not as unheard of as we might believe. (J.S. Davies, *A History of Southampton*, Southampton, 1883, p.458)

FEBRUARY 11TH

1808: On this day the stage coach from Salisbury was delayed for six hours, not arriving until 12.30 instead of 6p.m.

The reason for the delay was the weather, described as a tempest and a fall of snow. Trees had blown down and had fallen across the road, blocking the coach until they were sawn up and removed. At the same time, the Itchen Ferry crossing was closed due to the wind, something that had not happened for many years. As part of the same report, it is recorded that many people had come to the town that week for 'the dipping in the salt water for the bite of mad dogs' and had 'returned home in better spirits'. Apparently, not even snow and tempests could put off those determined to get a cure. (*Hampshire Telegraph & Sussex Chronicle*, 15 February 1808)

February 12th

1921: On this day, two letters requesting separation allowance from the army were reported.

The British Army were on duty in Ireland and, as was usual, wives and dependants of soldiers were entitled to a direct payment from the army. This was the separation allowance and was intended to ensure the men's families had adequate means of support during their absence abroad. Payment, however, was not always as prompt as the women would have wished, and they were often obliged to write to the authorities. In an age when getting an education was still rather variable, women could still be almost illiterate; dealing with officialdom could therefore be a rather daunting experience for them. These two ladies had done their best, but achieved some ambiguous results.

Dear Sir,
Owing to your delay in sending me my money, we have not a morsel of food in the house. Hoping you are the same.
Yours etc.

Dear Sir,
If you do not send me my husband's money I shall have to lead an immortal life.
Yours etc.

(*Southern Daily Echo*)

FEBRUARY 13TH

1609: On this day chimneys were a concern for the authorities.
In a community where nearly all the houses were timber-framed, the fear of fire was very real, especially in tradesmen's workshops and businesses like bakeries and blacksmiths. In uncleaned chimneys, the accumulated soot inside was likely to catch alight if the fire in the hearth got too fierce. Two residents had allowed this to happen and were called to account. Thomas Michell lived in St Michael's parish and his chimney had caught fire in the night. He was fined 3s 4d (17p). The clerk adds the comment, 'All be it, he ought to pay six and eightpence.' In other words, he'd got off lightly! The second offender was Essay Whittiffe, a constant nuisance to the authorities. His chimney had been alight around midnight and he had been told to attend today, but 'he did not now appeere'. I doubt if anyone was surprised. (J. Horrocks, *Assembly Books of Southampton, Vol. II*, Southampton, 1920, p.19)

———— ◆ ————

1841: On this day the royal baptism was celebrated by bell-ringing and flags on nearly every building; a 'feeling of loyalty and affection prevailed ... all cried 'God bless her!'. (*Hampshire Advertiser & Salisbury Guardian*, 13 February 1841, Issue 917)

FEBRUARY 14TH

1980: On this day local councillors were in training for a sports competition, which would be held at Eastleigh. Teams from sports clubs, local firms and stores would be competing. The sports in the competition included: badminton, bowls, squash, swimming, table tennis and a general fitness competition! (*Southern Daily Echo*)

FEBRUARY 15TH

1572: On this day, Peter Chamberlen the younger was born in Southampton, where he lived with his parents and siblings until the 1590s.

The family had a medical background and Peter became a barber-surgeon, holding a bishop's licence to practise. He worked with his brother, Peter the elder, frequently pushing against the boundaries between surgery and medicine. Peter the elder was once imprisoned in Newgate for impinging on the physicians' territory. He was released after intervention by the Archbishop of Canterbury. Unusually for the time, the brothers concerned themselves with obstetrical matters and were referred to as 'man-midwives'. Such was their fame and skill that the elder brother received a diamond ring from Queen Anne in 1614. The eldest son of Peter the younger was recorded as being fond of using 'iron instruments' in difficult births. The midwifery tradition was passed down for another two generations, before it was broken. By then, it was accepted that the Chamberlens had developed the first obstetrical forceps. This seems to have been confirmed when, in 1815, Peter the younger's own instruments were discovered under the floorboards of the house, where he died in 1626 at Downe in Kent. (Dictionary of National Biography online)

February 16th

1934: On this day it was announced that the Thorners Charity Almshouses in Above Bar would be demolished as soon as the last residents could be moved to the new buildings in Regents Park Road.

The site would be taken over by Associated British Cinemas (ABC) to build a new super-cinema seating 2,000 people. Two years would be allowed for the company to build the cinema and make the necessary improvements to the roads in the area. During that time ABC would only pay a peppercorn rent, but at the end of two years they would pay an annual rent of £4,000. An alternative plan had been discussed, in which the open space created by the demolition of the almshouses would be retained in order to improve the view of the Guildhall, and the vista from the building itself. This had been rejected because it would have meant a loss of income for the Corporation. (*Southern Daily Echo*, 16 February 1934)

FEBRUARY 17TH

1609: On this day, Hugh New was again complaining about Judith Brading's behaviour towards him.

The week before, she had acted most contritely and begged forgiveness from him, and the town authorities, for her slanderous accusations against him. Moreover, she had promised to leave the town, but had remained and was still publicly abusing him, accusing him of having 'burned her with a filthy disease'. Her punishment was now to be made public and she was to be shut in the town cage, with a paper attached to her proclaiming her crime: 'For slanderous and reproachful words.' The matter rumbled on, with New renewing his complaint on 10 March when she was to be whipped – when she could be found. When she was found, she was put in the cage again, but not whipped. Her last appearance before the authorities was as a complainant. The record states: 'Judith Brading, great with child came to the house, alleging Richard Greenaway ... to be the father thereof. Order is to be given to the constable for his apprehension.' (J. Horrocks, *Assembly Books of Southampton, 1609-1610*, Southampton, 1920, pp.13, 24, 29, 68)

FEBRUARY 18TH

1924: On this day it was reported that the shortage of rabbits in the east of the county was possibly due to a plague of rats, which were destroying the young in their nests. In some areas, both hedgerows and fields were swarming with rats.

It seems likely that the plague was caused by voles, not rats. Voles regularly have population explosions and the rabbits were probably suffering from a lack of food due to the competition from the voles, with the result that the rabbits could not breed as quickly as usual. (*Southern Daily Echo*, 18 February 1924)

FEBRUARY 19TH

1980: On this day, with the approach of Shrove Tuesday, a new recipe for pancake batter was published, which sounds very tempting – the batter was mixed with a tot of Southern Comfort. It appears to be an American recipe because all the measurements are given as tablespoons. It still sounds good! So here it is:

    5 tablespoons of plain flour
    1 tablespoon of icing sugar
    1 egg and a pinch of salt
    2 tablespoons of melted butter
    2 tablespoons of Southern Comfort
    Single cream or milk to mix and make the usual batter
    consistency
    Cook the pancakes in the usual way and serve traditionally with
    lemon and sugar, alternatively serve with fruit and a drizzle of
    Southern Comfort.

Southern Comfort was devised in the Deep South of America after the Civil War. Traditionally it is a blend of oranges, peaches and other fruit and herbs. The recipe is supposed to run to over 100 pages! Here's to a merry Shrove Tuesday! (*Southern Daily Echo*)

FEBRUARY 20TH

1663: On this day there was a 'mutiny' amongst the poor due to the scarcity of affordable bread.

The Mayor sent for the bakers and millers and, in the presence of the justices, offered them good wheat at a favourable rate. He promised to fix the price until the harvest, on condition that the millers and bakers began work quickly and held their bread prices down until midsummer. He promised a rent-free storehouse and, anticipating they would be unable to pay for any delivery immediately, he offered to give them an extended period for payment. Under the eyes of the trained bands, the millers and bakers obligingly accepted the terms. The Mayor's quick action and readily available supply of wheat must give rise to the suspicion that originally he had intended to make a profit on the stored wheat, as the price rose during the shortage. Perhaps the poor knew of the stockpile, hence the riot. (J.S. Davies, *A History of Southampton*, Southampton, 1883, pp.265, 495)

FEBRUARY 21ST

1934: On this day it was reported that RMS *Olympic* would be taking £5 million worth of gold bullion to New York. Approximately one half of it would be taken on at Cherbourg the same evening.

———•◆•———

1934: On this day the local entertainments pages confirmed that Sotonians could enjoy a wide variety of activities to amuse themselves. These included greyhound racing at the stadium; three dances at local ballrooms; live theatre performances at the Grand Theatre, Palace Theatre and Hippodrome; and a choice of eleven cinemas (including the Empire – now the Mayflower Theatre), each one providing a programme consisting of two films, a newsreel, cartoons and an interval in which an organist played various popular tunes for the audience. For those who wished to travel it was possible to go to the Newbury races by coach for 5s 6d (27p) return, or even go by train to Cardiff for 7s (35p) return. For the more seriously minded inhabitants there was a Grand Public meeting on Fascism. (*Southern Daily Echo*, 21 February 1934)

FEBRUARY 22ND

1928: On this day the Hamble-based pilot, Bert Hinkler, completed his marathon solo flight from England to Australia – the first person to do so.

Hinkler was a test pilot at Hamble, respected for his technical skill and unassuming manner. His modesty, however, was an impediment when seeking financial sponsorship for his various long-distance flights. He financed them all from his savings. For the epic Australian flight he chose a Hamble-built Avro Avian, which he maintained himself each evening on the journey, and frequently slept beneath its wings. It took fifteen and a half days altogether, in sixteen 'legs', before he finally arrived in Darwin. Eight years earlier he had taken his old Avro Baby biplane to Australia and flown it non-stop 700 miles from Sydney to his hometown of Bundaberg, taxiing up the main street to stop outside his mother's house! Hinkler went to Canada in 1931 to complete more solo feats in a Puss Moth, eventually flying from Brazil across the Atlantic to Africa, twenty-two hours non-stop. He flew back to London then, escorted by planes from Hamble, on to Eastleigh, to be met by Councillor Fred Woolley, Mayor of Southampton. (A.G.K. Leonard, *Stories of Southampton Streets*, Southampton, 1984, pp.106-10)

FEBRUARY 23RD

1757: On this day, John de la Mere fell from the town walls whilst being chased by the press gang; he died.

De la Mere was a Guernsey seaman and therefore should have been exempt from serving in the British Navy – but this was early in the Seven Years War and, in 1757, a 'heavy press' had been imposed on the town. As was usual when the press gang was expected, most of the local men aged between fifteen and fifty had managed to make themselves scarce by leaving the town. De la Mere, believing himself safe by his exemption, did not return to his own ship and stayed in the town. Seeing a likely victim, the press gang descended upon the unlucky man, who ran away and jumped over an apparently low portion of the town wall. Unfortunately, being a stranger in the town, he was unaware that this section of wall was actually built against the high gravel bank. On the other side was a 50ft drop to the beach. He broke his neck. (St Michael's parish burial registers)

FEBRUARY 24TH

1940: On this day, the following useful hints were produced as the beginning of what would become the 'Make do and Mend' campaign.

1) A teaspoonful of lemon juice added to a tin of metal polish will keep metal objects cleaner longer.

2) Old water bottles stuffed with soft rags make good kneeling mats.

3) Methylated spirits added to the rinsing water for silk stockings stop them getting stained in the rain.

4) If a carving knife stands in boiling water before use, it gives a smoother, easier cut, and therefore thinner slices of meat.

5) Before using a new packet of tea, spread the contents out on brown paper and place in a warm oven for ten minutes. It will give a better flavour and go twice as far. (*Hampshire Advertiser & Southampton Times*, 24 February 1940)

FEBRUARY 25TH

1928: On this day the world's largest liner, the White Star Line *Majestic* (56,551 tons), was just finishing her overhaul and refit, which had included two days in the world's largest floating dock at Southampton.

The interior had been considerably improved, and good taste, together with the maximum in comfort, was apparent everywhere on the ship. In particular, the Third Class accommodation had been greatly improved due to its increased popularity with the travelling public – the tourists. New facilities included the installation of a new lounge, writing room and reading room, which had all been furnished with a great deal of wicker furniture. A new ballroom floor had been installed, and in future it would be possible to dance on the deck thanks to the extension of the ship's panatrope system (the phonograph or gramophone amplification system). (*Southern Daily Echo*, 25 February 1928)

FEBRUARY 26TH

1618: On this day, a letter from the court at Whitehall was received, acknowledging receipt of just over £92 from the merchants and ship-owners of Southampton, as a donation to help suppress pirates at sea, especially those of Algiers and Tunis.

However, the Lords of the council were not pleased because they had already written to the town requesting that it donate £300 over the next two years. Ninety-two pounds was not enough; they wanted another £58 to make the first instalment up to £150. The Mayor was not to be bullied. He wrote back a few days later with a further £8, which the merchants were donating 'for the full service'. More pressure was put on the Corporation by the Lords and eventually the town paid up the rest of the first instalment. After all this argument, the King decided to put off the expedition to suppress the pirates, and the £150 was returned to the town. (J.C. Jeaffreson, *The Manuscripts of the Corporations of Southampton and King's Lynn*, 1887, pp.130-1)

FEBRUARY 27TH

1921: On this day, the troopship *Huntspill* mysteriously sank in Southampton Docks.

An ex-German passenger ship, she was moored north of the Cold Store and, at about 8 p.m., water suddenly began to pour into the ship, making it list badly to port. Since most of the portholes were open, as the ship began to tilt these became submerged and even more water poured in, filling the hold and engine rooms. There were only a few crew members on board and they could do little to rescue the ship. The result was inevitable. She sank and came to rest on the mud.

The ship had been scheduled to carry troops to Bombay the following day and all their stores on board had been lost in the sinking. It was subsequently found that a combination of circumstances had caused the accident; some repairs to the ship had meant that the hole in the hull, for the ash-ejector, had not been covered over. This, coupled with uneven ballast distribution, resulted in the fateful inrush of water. She was successfully raised, sold and returned to passenger service in Asia, eventually being broken up in 1933. (A.G.K. Leonard, *Journal of the Southampton Local History Forum*, Winter 2008; *Southern Daily Echo*, 28 February 1921)

February 28th

1924: On this day, the Automobile Association's (AA) innovative signposting scheme met with considerable public approval. The AA had fixed direction signs onto the tram standards in various parts of the town. These gave directions not only to distant parts of the country 'but also instruct[ed] the traveller in reaching the extremities of the boroughs'.

———— • ◆ • ————

1924: On this day, a letter reported that a pair of watercolour drawings of the Southampton Bargate and the Westgate, each 0.5in square, together with another of the Great Exhibition in Hyde Park (measuring 0.5in by 1in), all made by George Day of Wilton Avenue, had been accepted by Her Royal Highness Princess Marie for the royal dolls' house. (*Southern Daily Echo*, 28 February 1924)

FEBRUARY 29TH

1952: On this day a court case was brought against Mr Leslie Tracy, for causing an obstruction in East Street.

Mr Tracy was an upholsterer and had been making an armchair, as a demonstration, in the window of his shop in East Street. Twenty-two interested people had gathered on the pavement to watch him at work. The local 'Bobby on the Beat', PC Carter, considered that this number of people was causing an obstruction for other pedestrians. Mr Tracy thought that he was on his own premises and, therefore, could do as he pleased. During the court case, the upholsterer pointed out that he had been demonstrating in his window for the last fifty-seven days and, during that time, approximately 100 police constables must have passed by, but had not considered his activity unusual. Was only PC Carter right and all the other officers wrong? Incredibly, the magistrates adjourned the case for a week to consider their verdict, but it wasn't reported in the local paper afterwards. We will never know if Mr Tracy continued to work in the window of his shop or not, but the firm flourished for many more years. (*Southern Daily Echo*)

MARCH 1ST

1921: On this day, Mayor Blatch wrote a letter to the *Echo* praising the work of the Southampton Record Society in producing books of the town's civic records.

The work, he said, was carried on by 'a small number of ladies and gentlemen, who not only pay their subscriptions but give the labour of their years voluntarily'. The *Athenaeum* said that 'all old towns should have active Record Societies like Southampton'. The documents were a rich record of the town's medieval history and the journal, *English Historical Review*, considered that valuable town records would rarely be copied or published if it were not for the self-denying labours of the local scholars. The SRS had been set up in 1905 and produced a volume each year, until the Second World War, when all its remaining stock of printed volumes was lost in the Blitz. There was some discussion about whether to continue or not after such a setback, but, rising like the phoenix from the ashes, the work continued jointly under the auspices of the City Council and the University of Southampton. To denote the changed circumstances, the name became Southampton Records Series and the books changed colour from green to blue bindings, with the first volume appearing in 1951. It continues to publish regularly in 2012. (*Southern Daily Echo*, 1 March 1912; M. South, 'The Southampton Records Series', *Local History News*, No. 98)

MARCH 2ND

1984: On this day, notice was given that the South of England Majorettes Championship would again be sponsored by the *Southern Daily Echo*.

The decision had been taken following the success of the previous year's inaugural event. Officially called Marching Bands, the competition was scheduled to take place between 8 and 12 August. It would comprise two sections: novice (for those who had never won a competition) and an open class for the top troupes in the area. Details of arrangements and the timetable for the heats were provided, though it was stated that these might have to be changed according to the number of entries for the contest. (*Southern Daily Echo*, 2 March 1984)

MARCH 3RD

1926: On this day the first Southampton Music Festival was declared a wonderful success.

The festival took place over four days and the Grand Finale/Concert and presentation of the trophies took place at the Coliseum at the end of the week. Over 2,000 people had taken part with over 850 entries in sixty-six different classes. The solo piano class was the most popular, with more than 300 competitors. Not many choirs took part, although these were from a wide variety of groups, including school choirs, separate boys' and girls' choirs, and several church choirs. Solo lady vocalists were well represented and there was one event which may seem surprising in a music festival – an elocution competition. No doubt it was considered necessary training for all singers at the time. The organisers were delighted with the overall response, the standard of the entries and the interest of the public. They were looking forward to an even better event next year ... and the next, and the one after that, then the following year ... until 2012, when the event now extends over two weekends and two other days. Elocution has disappeared to be replaced by an extensive drama section instead. (*Hampshire Advertiser & Southampton Times*, 3 March 1926)

MARCH 4TH

1929: On this day, Hampshire Aeroplane Club at Hamble recorded a total flying time of fourteen hours, fifteen minutes. One member of the club had completed his tests and obtained his 'A' licence – the first this year.

The Avian aircraft had returned ... 'and the undercarriage should be very popular. It seems to [with]stand a vertical landing from about two hundred feet. Members are not recommended to try it, however, as the Chief Instructor's nerves are not as strong as the undercarriage'. (*Southern Daily Echo*, 4 March 1929)

MARCH 5TH

1936: On this day, the first flight of the VS300 aircraft No. K5054 took place at Southampton airport. The Spitfire had taken to its natural element – the air.

The Supermarine Aviation Works had been situated alongside the River Itchen since 1913, eventually being taken over by Vickers – hence the VS300 designation for the aircraft type. In 1934 the company's designer, R.J. Mitchell, was authorised to design a completely new fighter aeroplane free from official specifications. He did. The Spitfire broke most of the rules with its revolutionary thin, elliptically shaped wings, containing an eight-gun battery, the enclosed cockpit and its retractable undercarriage. The test flight report was brief; Captain Joseph 'Mutt' Summers said, 'Don't change anything!' A legend had been born, but unfortunately Mitchell himself was never to see how important the Spitfire's role would become during the Battle of Britain, nor how it attained its iconic status; he died in 1937, having lived long enough to see the first production model fly in 1936.

The aeroplane had been christened Spitfire by the Chairman of the Board. Mitchell thought it was 'bloody silly'. Probably the only mistake he made about the plane. (C.F. Andrews and E.B. Morgan, *Supermarine Aircraft Since 1914*, London, 1981)

MARCH 6TH

1873: On this day Charles Fryatt was baptised at St Mary's Church and was destined to follow in his father's footsteps to become a mariner.

When his father joined the Great Eastern Railway, Charles did likewise and worked his way up to become a ship's master in 1913, taking command of the SS *Brussels* in 1914. He operated the unarmed merchant vessel on a service between Harwich and Holland, which was neutral. Fryatt had several notable encounters with enemy warships and submarines, managing to elude or outrun them by his superior seamanship. In March 1915 he sighted one of the new U-boats approaching his ship and boldly ordered full speed ahead towards the submarine, forcing it to submerge. Fryatt then brought his ship safely to Rotterdam. The publicity surrounding him made Fryatt an enemy target and his ship was captured in June 1916. He was court-martialled at Bruges, sentenced to death and shot an hour later. Fryatt's body was returned to England and a memorial service held at St Paul's Cathedral on 8 July 1919. A commemoration plaque was unveiled at Freemantle School (which he attended as a child) in 2007. (A.G.K. Leonard, *Journal of the Southampton Local History Forum*, Autumn 2011)

MARCH 7TH

1644: On this day there was a confrontation between the Cavaliers and Roundheads.

A force of Royalist soldiers from Winchester, led by Lord Hopton, came and faced the town. Colonel Norton (aiding Murford, the Parliamentarian Governor of Southampton) sent some troops out to engage the Royalists, but also sent others out by a longer route to ambush them from the rear. It was a decisive action with disastrous results for the Royalists. Estimates of those killed or taken prisoner were between eighty and 140, while eyewitnesses claimed to have seen five cartloads of dead being taken away. Eighty horses and some officers were taken to Southampton, while Norton's losses were given as three.

During the Civil War Southampton had become a Parliamentarian garrison, despite being almost completely surrounded by communities sympathetic to the Royalist cause. There were frequent skirmishes and breakouts from the town for food, but this seems to have been a genuine engagement for once. (*Mercurius Civicus Londons Intelligencer*, 7-14 March 1644, Issue 42; G.N. Godwin, *The Civil War in Hampshire*, Alresford, 1973, p.169)

MARCH 8TH

1928: On this day, floating bridge *No. 7* was sunk. At 4 p.m., *No. 7* left the Woolston side of the River Itchen and headed for the town centre on the other side. The underpowered tug *Fawley* was coming downriver, riding on a fast-ebb tide and towing a barge full of refuse. Mid-river, the *Fawley's* bows struck the floating bridge squarely in the engine room, breaking one of the cables. Locked together, they started to drift downstream; with *No. 7's* other cable running free, the bridge was out of control.

People on shore had watched the slow-motion collision taking place and now responded to the *Fawley's* blasts of alarm. Cutting her barge free, the tug managed to extricate herself from the floating bridge and returned to start taking passengers off *No. 7*, which was sinking. At the same time, two tugs came from the coal jetty and tried to secure the floating bridge, while launches, dinghies and rowing boats converged from all sides, to take the sixty or more passengers off. All efforts to move the bridge failed; she sank midstream about twenty minutes after the impact and shortly after the last passengers had been rescued. (J. Horne, *Farewell to the Floating Bridges*, Southampton, 1977)

MARCH 9TH

1901: On this day the Saints Football Club played their first international match (against Ireland) at their new ground, the Dell.

The legendary all-round sportsman Charles Burgess Fry, already an amateur athletics international, played for the Saints as full-back, and this match gave him full international honours for England. The following year he played for Southampton in the Cup Final, against Sheffield United at Crystal Palace. Two days later, Fry was playing cricket for the London counties (against Surrey) at the Oval, when he made eighty-two runs. It was for his prowess as a cricketer that C.B. Fry is chiefly remembered, still playing for Hampshire in 1912, aged forty. The statistics surrounding his cricketing career are impressive; he scored 30,886 runs, including ninety-four centuries. Apart from his local involvement with football and cricket, Fry is also remembered for his involvement with the training ship *Mercury*, moored in the River Hamble. Boys and young men were trained for the navy under the auspices of Fry and his wife Beatrice. Mrs Fry was considered to be a harder disciplinarian than Fry himself. (*Southern Daily Echo*, 10 March 1901; Dictionary of National Biography online)

March 10th

1903: On this day, permission was sought by stonemasons Garret and Haysom to 'place a cattle trough on Western Esplanade, on the site of Madame Maes house'. The council's Works Committee agreed to the suggestion, 'subject to the trough being erected to the satisfaction of the Borough Engineer'.

Madame Maes had been the last occupant of the house, and after her death the house was demolished in order to extend Western Esplanade, making access to the Royal Pier and Terminus railway station easier. Madame Maes (the title was adopted because she married a Frenchman) and her children lived in the house for twenty-five years. She was a popular and generous lady, known to have given away even some of the clothes she was wearing. The grounds of the house were opened up to provide a playground for local children, where the old mulberry tree was especially loved for climbing. The trough, which was only used for horses, is now a Grade II listed building situated near the Mayflower Memorial. (A.G.K. Leonard, 'Westgate House and Madame Maes', *Journal of the Southampton Local History Forum*, Winter 2003; http://www.southampton.gov.uk/Images/Westgate)

MARCH 11TH

1607: On this day Richard Anderson was brought to the Assembly, having run away from his master, Mr Hoskins.

It was usual for orphans to be placed in the care of a family, who were paid an allowance by the town to foster the child until he/she was old enough to be apprenticed. Richard had been cared for by Thomas Buckett and his wife for ten years, in the village of Nursling, at the expense of Southampton. He had been apprenticed to Mr Hoskins, a glover living in the parish of All Saints. Hoskins had been paid £1 for the boy's apprenticeship, which would last seven years. But after one week Richard had run away and returned to the Bucketts at Nursling. Hoskins was described as a 'poore man ... not of habilitie to maintain him [Richard]' and it was stated that he should release the boy and repay half of the money he had received. Hoskins was unable to do this and so was sent to the Bargate Gaol until he could repay the money. Richard returned to the Bucketts, who promised the Assembly that they would find a good master for him in the country. (J. Horrocks, *Assembly Books of Southampton, Vol. I, 1602-1608*, Southampton, 1917, pp.52-3)

MARCH 12TH

1349: On this day, Adam de Sunnynges was appointed the new vicar for the parish of Holy Rood, after the death of the previous incumbent.

When de Sunnynges died, just a few weeks later, the vacancy was filled by Henry de Chippenham, on 22 April 1349. Henry managed to survive until the end of the summer and then, on 20 September 1349, John de Upton became vicar. The reason for the high death rate was the notorious Black Death which, according to Henry Knighton, a contemporary chronicler at Leicester, had first entered England via Southampton. He recorded that 'the most lamentable plague penetrated the coast through Southampton' during the summer of 1348. Nearly half the clergy died during the outbreak, which lasted throughout 1348 and 1349. Mortality figures are notoriously difficult to estimate, but it is now generally understood that approximately two-thirds of the entire population perished. This seems to accord with the inscription in Ashwell Church in Hertfordshire, which says that only 'the dregs of the populace live to tell the tale'. (T.B. James, *The Black Death in Hampshire*, Hampshire, 1999, p.2; C. Platt, *Medieval Southampton*, London, 1973, p.120)

MARCH 13TH

1474: On this day, John Sexton of Bishopstoke came to the Common Court to complain against Thomas Brasiar.

Brasiar was holding two brass pots belonging to Sexton (surely their names reflect their trades). One weighed 27lb and the other weighed 3lb. The total valuation was disputed, but Brasiar admitted he had them. The case appears to have been brought before the court on an earlier occasion, because Sexton had been given leave previously to seize his property. He had obviously not been successful. Sexton was again given leave to get his goods from Brasiar, who was now fined 3*d* for unlawful detention (of the pots) and put in gaol 'until he should provide satisfaction'. It appears that this was meant to give Sexton an opportunity to regain his pots while Brasiar was in gaol, and Brasiar would be kept there until Sexton had retrieved them. (T. Olding, *The Common and Piepowder Courts of Southampton, 1426-1483*, Southampton, 2011, Part I, p.26)

MARCH 14TH

1877: On this day, General Juan Manuel de Rosas died after twenty-six years' exile in Southampton.

De Rosas was born in Argentina and had a meteoric rise to power and infamy. He became Governor of Buenos Aires in 1829 and was regarded as an energetic reformer. He resigned from office in 1832 to conquer more lands. Three years later, he returned a national hero and became Governor of Buenos Aires again. Now he began to show his true colours. The first famous incident recorded was when he ordered the death of his prisoners, while cutting the throat of a twelve-year-old child. His reign of terror was maintained by his death squads on the streets, and continued for seventeen years. Eventually the ranch owners (originally his allies) ousted him and he fled to exile in England, settling in Southampton. Here he became viewed as an eccentric figure, riding around the town on his black horse, wearing a black cape and flat black gaucho hat. On his death he was buried in the Old Cemetery on the Common. In 1989, after diplomatic relations with Argentina had been reinstated following the Falklands War, his remains were quietly exhumed and returned. (History of Argentina online; Friends of Southampton Old Cemetery)

MARCH 15TH

1781: On this day, John Speed MD died. He was buried two days later in Holy Rood Church.

Although he was a physician and probably treated many of the town's fashionable spa visitors at this time, he is better known for his work compiling a coherent history of the town. This was a ground-breaking effort, working his way through the town's old charters and miscellaneous civic documents to produce his manuscript, 'History and Antiquities of Southampton'. This was published by the Southampton Records Series in 1909, as one of their first volumes. Notwithstanding his scholarship, Speed was equally well known for his strong viewpoint, and outspoken attacks on the Corporation and its visitors. Oxford University, where he studied medicine, tended to resist scientific innovation and this attitude seems to have influenced some of Speed's strong opinions; he appears to have been suspicious of new medical approaches, especially those of the surgeons. He stopped his servant being inoculated against smallpox and apparently disinherited his daughter Elizabeth because she desired 'to marry a person of whom I very much disapprove'. The 'person' was the surgeon and apothecary George Goring. After Speed's death, Elizabeth's brother made financial arrangements for her. (Dictionary of National Biography online)

MARCH 16TH

1776: On this day, Nathaniel St Andre was buried.

Born in Switzerland, he had been appointed surgeon to George I in 1723. However, he later lost credibility due to a series of notorious incidents, the most famous being the 'Rabbit Woman of Godalming'. In 1726, Mary Toft, an agricultural worker, began telling stories about being startled by a rabbit while she was pregnant. The story turned into a hoax when she apparently started giving birth to rabbits. St Andre was duped and wrote a treatise about the case, which was published. When Toft admitted the hoax, he became a laughing stock. Scandal struck again when his friend, the MP Samuel Molyneux, became ill in Parliament. St Andre was called to treat him, but Molyneux died a few days later. St Andre eloped with Molyneux's wife, Elizabeth, that very night. He was accused of poisoning Molyneux, but won his case for defamation and married Elizabeth in 1730. They retired to Southampton in the early 1750s, living in the High Street near the Dolphin Hotel. In 1768 he built Bellevue House, south of the Avenue. After Elizabeth died, her money went elsewhere and he lived in poverty until his death. He did not eat rabbit for over fifty years. (Holy Rood parish registers; Dictionary of National Biography online; L. Cody, *Birthing the Nation*, Oxford, 2005, pp.120-44)

MARCH 17TH

1974: On this day the new Southampton College of Art and Printing was opened as the modern replacement for the first School of Art, founded in 1855.

The original school was one of the first established after the Great Exhibition of 1851, when the Prince Consort appealed for Schools of Art to be established throughout England. Southampton's was set up in the Royal Victoria Assembly Rooms and then moved to the Civic Centre in 1938. The following year, the art gallery was opened. During a 1940 air raid the School of Art took a direct hit, with some loss of life. After this setback it seemed as if the city might lose its art school, until plans were made to establish a new College of Art, now Solent University. Although there are no great artistic names associated with Southampton, paintings from the early artists of the school were collected by Robert Chipperfield, a London pharmacist who moved to Southampton in 1842. He bequeathed these to the city, together with enough money to set up an art gallery. His bequest formed the basis of the city's art collection and shows the high standards achieved by the School of Art's students, some of whom exhibited in London. (Anne Anderson, 'All Roads Lead to London, or Elsewhere', M. Taylor (ed.), *Southampton: Gateway to the British Empire*, London, 2007; Friends of Southampton Old Cemetery Newsletter, September 2008)

March 18th

1747: On this day, Mr Voier was travelling by coach from Southampton to London when the coach was held up by a highwayman.

Threatening Mr Voier with two pistols, the highwayman demanded all his money. When he found that this only amounted to 14s, he obviously thought an attempt had been made to hide other money in the coach, and ordered Mr Voier to get out while he searched the seats. This was a tactical error. While he was carrying out the search Mr Voier hit him over the head, took away the pistols and, together with the coachman, trussed him up and took him off to the local constable. (*Morning Advertiser*, Issue 606)

MARCH 19TH

1921: On this day, an article on the arrival of the first kite was published.

This was a species that only appeared in the spring and it would not be long before the mature kite with its varied plumage, powerful wings and very long tail made its appearance. Sadly, some poor specimens had already been spotted trapped in the branches of the trees in Andrews Park. It was estimated that the kite season came roughly between tops and marbles, or maybe hoops and hopscotch. In the past, even adults had been seen flying kites in the parks or even on the Common. With the activity becoming so popular, it was suggested that a kite-flying club should be set up and a properly organised kite-flying festival held on the Common. (*Southern Daily Echo*, 19 March 1921)

MARCH 20TH

1827: On this day, a Grand Ball and Supper was held at the Dolphin Assembly Rooms.

Gone were the strict rules of the eighteenth century, when events were under the command of the Master of Ceremonies; instead, the proceedings were directed by six lady patronesses and six gentlemen stewards. As was usual in nineteenth-century news reports, the status of those attending was the first consideration, with 'all the rank and fashion of the neighbourhood to the amount of upwards 300 families' being present. The need for good taste was stressed, with the Ballroom being 'splendidly illuminated and tastefully decorated with artificial flowers'. New dances (a set of quadrilles) were danced to music from a London production, played by a band from London. Supper was served at two o'clock, which must be taken as 2 a.m., which was then followed by dancing of a more spirited nature until a late hour, when the company broke up 'highly gratified by their evening's entertainment'. (*Morning Post*, 22 March 1827)

MARCH 21ST

1552: On this day, Sir Richard Lyster resigned his office as Lord Chief Justice of England and retired to Tudor House, where he spent the last two years of his life. He died in March 1554 and was buried in St Michael's Church, opposite his house.

Lyster had been involved in some of the most momentous events in English history. His legal background and expertise saw him involved with the trial of Sir Thomas More, leading up to the establishment of Henry VIII as head of the English Church. He served as a member of the Grand Juries that sentenced Thomas More and Bishop Fisher to death. These events were closely linked to the King's divorce from Catherine of Aragon and his marriage to Anne Boleyn. Henry VIII is reputed to have come to Southampton and discussed the divorce with Lyster at Tudor House. Lyster was also present in Anne Boleyn's procession when she went to Westminster Hall for her Coronation in 1533. In 1567, Lyster's widow, Elizabeth, erected a canopied monument to him in St Michael's Church. Here his effigy still lies, wearing the robes of his legal profession. (Dictionary of National Biography online; Guide book to Tudor House, Southampton, 1954)

MARCH 22ND

1794: On this day, three French officers were landed at Southampton from St Malo.

Being Royalists, they were probably in some danger from the revolutionary bodies in France and the threat of the guillotine literally hung over their heads! Having now reached England they headed for London as quickly as possible, with intelligence for the government which was believed to be of utmost importance to England. Southampton was at the forefront of military and naval activities against France at this time, with transports for the troops moored in the waterways and military camps set up all round the town on the common lands. One visitor to the town remarked that 'we never saw a place that had such a military appearance as Southampton'. (*London Chronicle*, 1794; R. Douch, *Visitors' Descriptions of Southampton, 1540-1956*, Southampton, 1978, p.22)

MARCH 23RD

1539: On this day, Abbot John Bradley was consecrated as Suffragan Bishop of Shaftesbury at the little church of St John's in Southampton. John Capon, Bishop of Bangor, performed the consecration, assisted by John, Bishop of Hippo, and Thomas, Suffragan Bishop of Marlborough. Why this church was chosen for the consecration is unknown. It may be that there was a link with the Florentine community, which favoured this area of the town and bestowed the church with generous gifts.

A Florentine merchant dying in the town in 1466 bestowed gifts not only to the St John's vicar and clerk, but also towards the fabric of the church building. The following year, in 1467, the captain and patrons of the Florentine galley fleet, together with local Florentines, donated a whole set of tapestry curtains to the church. (J.S. Davies, *A History of Southampton*, Southampton, 1883; A. Ruddock, *Italian Merchants and Shipping in Southampton 1270-1600*, Southampton, 1951; C. Platt, *Medieval Southampton*, London, 1973)

MARCH 24TH

1903: On this day the great illusionist and mystery performer, Prince Samouda from West Africa, gave an extraordinary exhibition of thought-reading at the Victoria Hall, Southampton.

Prince Samouda was described as a much-respected member of the Showman's Guild and seems to have lived up to his reputation. When he appeared at Southampton he was working with his English wife, Madge. He described himself as a magician exhibition and Madge as a 'second sight artist' – i.e. a fortune teller. He was a travelling showman appearing at fairgrounds with an attraction called 'The Egyptian Mystery Show'; this was considered to be even more popular than the fairground rides, and was the most visited attraction at the fairs. In 1909 he published a full-page advertisement in the *World's Fair* for his 'New Garden Game', which he considered to be superior to all his others. Unfortunately, there are no indications of the content of his shows; the only clue we have is that he was credited with introducing the game of Hoop-La. (*Southern Daily Echo*; South Manchester census: 1901 RG13/3695 22 126 33; Sheffield University: National Fairground Archive)

MARCH 25TH

1742: On this day Mrs Ballard, the wife of the Mayor, was buried in Holy Rood Church.

Her death was a classic example of the dangers that pregnant women faced from smallpox. This was a year when the smallpox virus was particularly widespread throughout the country, and Southampton was also obliged to take in sick and wounded soldiers, who were housed in temporary hospitals. A large part of the population was unhealthy at this time, and Mrs Ballard had not had smallpox previously, so was not immune to the virus.

When a pregnant woman caught the disease it was a 75 per cent certainty that she would die. Smallpox caused her to miscarry her unborn child and the virus also reduced her blood's clotting ability. This resulted in severe haemorrhaging after the miscarriage. Medical practice would have recommended bleeding as a cure, with inevitably disastrous results. The parish records show that women were aware of the risks and some crossed over the water to smaller communities to give birth during smallpox outbreaks. As for Mr Ballard, he never forgot the experience and, thirty years later, contributed regularly to the inoculation campaigns in the town. (*See* January 6th) (Holy Rood parish registers; M. South, 'The Southampton Inoculation Campaigns of the Eighteenth Century', unpublished PhD thesis, University of Winchester, 2010, p.46)

MARCH 26TH

1517: On this day the Corporation, led by Mayor John Perchard, passed a ruling to partially enclose the Saltmarsh. This proved to be a bad idea: the Saltmarsh was common land and enclosure would limit its use for the townspeople.

The following Tuesday happened to be the Lawday, or Court Leet, which the townspeople seem to have regarded as an opportunity to make their feelings known. About 300 men and women gathered on the Saltmarsh, and, using various tools, broke down the new banks and ditches before marching to the Bargate, where the court was taking place. Unable to gain access to the court (the entrance to the Town Hall, at the Bargate, was up an easily barred narrow staircase), they remained outside, making a great noise, shouting and waving their pikes and shovels, before eventually lining up, with their implements on their shoulders, and marching to the Mayor's house at Holy Rood. Mighill Bonany, one of the ringleaders, then shouted, 'Now if Master Mayor have any more work for us, we be here ready!' After that, they all dispersed. (*See* April 4th) (A. Merson, *The Third Book of Remembrance of Southampton, Vol. I*, Southampton, 1952, pp.20-6)

MARCH 27TH

1952: On this day the new ice rink and Sportsdrome opened after the destruction of the old one by a parachute bomb in 1940.

The first ice rink had opened in July 1931. In 1936, inspired by the success of the Great Britain ice-hockey team in the 1936 Olympics, the Southampton Vikings ice-hockey team came into being and played its first match that November. It was initially made up from the Club Francais Volants team that had collapsed due to crippling debts. Their team kit had been decorated with a 'V' and, in order to economise, it was decided to keep the kit and give the team a name beginning with V – hence the Vikings. After the ice rink's destruction, Charlie Knott, a local entrepreneur and ice-hockey enthusiast, vowed to build a new rink for the town. He obtained an ice plant from the Purley ice rink and a steel-structured building from Supermarine, and built the new rink on the site of the old Sportsdrome. The Vikings returned and enjoyed considerable success during the 1950s and early '60s, winning the British Ice Hockey Association Cup five times before the rink was closed in 1983. (http://www.southampton-vikings.co.uk/history.htm)

MARCH 28TH

1606: On this day the price of double-strength beer was set at 3s 4d the barrel and ordinary beer at 2s the barrel.

It was usual for the magistrates to set the prices of beer and bread according to prevailing conditions, which might include poor harvests of the crops needed. On this occasion the price of malt had risen; the brewers complained that they could not afford to sell ordinary beer for 1s 8d and asked for a price of 2s 4d to be fixed. The magistrates chose to fix the price exactly in the middle, trying to keep everybody happy. There were only to be six legal ale brewers in the town, who were required to live in convenient areas. Obviously these were thirsty people; the brewers were ordered to serve full measure quarts (two pints) indoors, but the outdoors measure was to be three pints for the price of two pints. 'Take-away' prices are nothing new! (J. Horrocks, *Assembly Books of Southampton, Vol. I, 1602-1608*, Southampton, 1917, p.40)

MARCH 29TH

1851: On this day the private yacht *Sea Dog* set sail from Southampton, intending to go to Yarmouth on the Isle of Wight.

The owner and his brother-in-law were on board, along with the captain. Near Calshot Castle they ran into a steamer, the *Duke of Buccleugh*, and the yacht immediately sank. The lifeboat on board was lowered successfully and the men – with the exception of Mr Barfoot (the owner's brother-in-law) – managed to get on board. Mr Barfoot unfortunately could not get into the boat and remained in the water, rapidly tiring. The steamer captain, Mr Gilpin, leapt into the water and supported him until they were all rescued by the boat and got onto the steamer. The steamer headed back to Southampton and medical aid was administered to Mr Barfoot, who was now recovering well after receiving the kind attentions of Mrs Quilter at the King's Arms Hotel. While this may not appear very newsworthy nowadays, it must be remembered that, at this time, few people were strong swimmers (if they swam at all) and windproof clothing was made of thick woollen fabric, which would be very heavy when wet and could drag a clothed man under the water very quickly. (*Daily News*, 29 March 1851)

MARCH 30TH

1899: On this day, the London & South Western Railway ferry, the SS *Stella*, set sail from Southampton for Guernsey. She ran into fog but still proceeded at full speed, running onto the Casquet Rocks at about 4 p.m. and sinking within ten minutes.

The *Stella* was scheduled to arrive at 5.30 p.m., exactly the same time as her Great Western Railway rival from Weymouth. Although subsequently it was shown that the two vessels were not racing one another, the suspicion remained. Captain Reeks, of the *Stella*, was blamed for maintaining full speed in fog. Of the 190 people on board, seventy-seven drowned, including the stewardess Mary Ann Rogers. The story of the Southampton heroine fired the imagination of the press. *The Times* reported how she had helped the women into the lifeboats, even giving up her own lifejacket for one. She had refused to take a place in the lifeboat, saying she might capsize it, and waved everyone off. She wished them 'Farewell and good cheer', then, raising her arms above her head and crying 'Lord have me', she disappeared under the waves. Her story prompted a number of memorials, the finest of which is opposite the Royal Pier in Southampton. (http://www.jakesimpkin.org)

MARCH 31ST

1570: On this day it was decided to build a new market house.

Inhabitants and visitors to the town's open-air markets were fed up, and complained bitterly about the poor facilities for both sellers and buyers. Goods were being spoiled by wind and rain, and the people got similarly soaked and uncomfortable; some were choosing not to attend the markets at all. The decision was made to erect a new building on the south side of the Audit House, outside Holy Rood Church but also in the middle of the High Street. The cost and the amounts of materials used suggest that this was a large, fully enclosed market place, adjacent to the existing building. Presumably the sellers either erected their own stalls within the building or permanent stalls were provided for their use. However it was organised, the building sounds remarkably like a Tudor shopping mall! And we thought we'd invented them. (A. Merson, *The Third Book of Remembrance of Southampton, Vol. II*, Southampton, 1955, p.111)

APRIL 1ST

1899: On this day there was a meeting of the Southampton School Board, which discussed some intriguing proposals.

The Board seemed to be more concerned about ill-disciplined teachers than pupils. They thought that teachers should continue filling in their time-books (time sheets), otherwise discipline would suffer. This seems to have been considered the best way to check teachers' abilities. The suggestion was made that schools should also operate on Sundays. Some schools already had some extra classes on Saturdays, so why not open on Sundays as well? The suggestion was then made that alcohol should be allowed on the premises during school concerts. All three proposals were lost: time-books were discontinued, schools did not open on Sundays and no alcohol was allowed on school premises at any time. (*Hampshire Advertiser*, 1 April 1899)

APRIL 2ND

1919: On this day, Daniel Beak VC was given the Freedom of the Borough.

Beak was born at St Denys in Southampton, educated at Taunton's School, and joined the Royal Navy Volunteer Reserve aged sixteen, becoming Petty Officer. After service during the Gallipoli evacuation, the remainder of the First World War was spent in France. The citation for his Victoria Cross is extraordinary: 'For conspicuous bravery and courageous leadership during a prolonged period of operations'. He led his men in attack, and, despite heavy machine-gun fire, captured four enemy positions. His fearless leadership resulted in the complete success of this operation, enabling other battalions to reach their objectives. Four days later, without a brigade commander, he reorganised the brigade under heavy gunfire and led his men with splendid courage to their objective. An attack having been held up, he and one runner rushed forward, successfully breaking up a nest of machine guns and bringing back several prisoners. His example instilled courage and confidence in his men, who resumed the advance under his leadership. On a subsequent occasion he displayed courage and powers of leadership in attack; his initiative, coupled with the confidence he inspired in all ranks, enabled his unit to advance, and contributed materially to the success of the Division in these operations. He died aged seventy-six in 1967. (Victoria Cross online; A. Rance, *Southampton: An Illustrated History*, Southampton, 1980, p.143)

APRIL 3RD

1908: On this day a stag was killed on Southampton Common for the last time.

Mr Willis-Fleming had invited the New Forest Deerhounds to meet at Chilworth Manor, where he entertained them all most generously. After setting off, they soon put up a large buck in the woods between Chilworth and Stoneham; the chase continued across Red Lodge and then down to the Common, where the stag was eventually killed near the cemetery gates. Possibly the most remarkable part of this episode is the amount of open countryside which still stretched northwards all around the town at this time. (*Southern Daily Echo*, 3 April 1908)

APRIL 4TH

1517: On this day the King sent Sir William Sands, from the King's Council, to take the leaders of the Saltmarsh riot to London to stand trial before Henry VIII himself.

The four men who had run away with Mighill Bonany could not be found. Six others were arrested instead – William Sheperd, Robert Parker, Robert Emery, William Bartlett, Mighill Mardew and Robert Sendall – and taken 'like prisoners … that is to say their legs bound with halters under the horses bellies'. When they appeared at the King's Council they were committed to the notorious Marshalsea Prison, in London, where they remained until the middle of July. Alarmed by this outcome, the original rioters rebuilt the banks and ditches they had destroyed, made promises to the Mayor not to disturb the peace again and pleaded for the return of the prisoners. Satisfied with this turn of events, the Mayor and Corporation then pleaded with the King's Council for the men's release. Bishop Fox, from Winchester, also wrote a letter pleading for the men, which Sir John Dawtrey (owner of Tudor House) took to Cardinal Wolsey. The letters achieved their purpose; the men were released and returned to Southampton to take up their various trades once more. (A. Merson, *The Third Book of Remembrance of Southampton, 1514-1602, Vol. I*, Southampton, 1952, pp.22-6)

APRIL 5TH

1879: On this day the Ancient Order of Foresters held their annual dinner, and afterwards expressed their concerns about the sewage problem in the town.

This was serious. There had been four cholera outbreaks between 1849 and 1866. However, the cost of tackling the problem was deterring the Corporation from doing anything. The Guano Company Ltd convinced the authorities in 1870 that they could solve the problem. They believed that costs could be covered by turning the sewage into fertiliser. A site in Northam was obtained, next to a main sewer discharging into the River Itchen. The company built large tanks and steam engines, and pumped the sewage into these. By adding a secret ingredient, they thought a rich fertiliser would be produced. It did not work. Apparently, Southampton produced the wrong sort of sewage – it was too wet! The site was sold – part to the London & South Western Railway, and the rest to the Southampton Gas Light & Coke Co.

———◆———

1879: On this day at the Quarter Sessions, William Allen (fifty-eight) and Thomas Berry (seventeen) were indicted for an attempt at an unnatural offence, but the Grand Jury returned 'No Bill' and they were released. 'No Bill' indicated that the jury considered there to be insufficient evidence. (*Hampshire Advertiser*, 5 April 1879)

APRIL 6TH

1738: On this day, John Barnes and Ann Petty were married at Pear Tree Church before departing for Georgia. Rather surprisingly, another twenty-five couples were also wed there before leaving for the colony.

James Oglethorpe had taken the first group of Georgian settlers in 1732 to found the new colony. He returned to England, seeking more manpower for the colony, and our group of emigrants appears to be part of the second wave that he took back. It was Oglethorpe's original idea for British debtors to be released from prison and sent to Georgia. Some proposed that this would rid Britain of its so-called undesirable elements – but it was Britain's 'worthy poor' that Oglethorpe wanted. In reality, few debtors went; most of the new settlers were poor English tradesmen and artisans, together with religious refugees. The colony's charter provided for acceptance of all religions except Catholicism, because the Spanish colony of Florida was 'next door' and this might provoke divided loyalties within the Georgians. On arrival, families received approximately fifty acres of land: one acre for a house and five acres for a garden; and a further forty-five acres away from the town for clearing and farming. Perhaps it was this promised land allocation for families that produced the mass marriages. (Pear Tree Church registers; A. Coombes and W. Coates, 'Oglethorpe and the Oglethorpe Oak', *Arnoldia*, Summer 1997, pp.25-30; Dictionary of National Biography online)

APRIL 7TH

1609: On this day, the Corporation ordered that the Watergate at the bottom of the town should be smartened up.

King James' coat of arms was to be painted and placed upon a frame, facing the sea, between the two lions. The whole area was to be improved. Arundel Tower was likely to fall down unless the bank underneath it was repaired, and St Michael's Prison had fallen down and should be rebuilt. It appears that the Corporation were preparing themselves for a possible royal visit that summer, and they expected the King might enter the town from the sea. He was staying at Beaulieu for the summer and it would be an easy matter to travel from there to Southampton; they were going to be prepared. There is no record of a royal visit that year, but hopefully the town was a bit smarter for a while. (J. Horrocks, *Assembly Books of Southampton, Vol. II, 1609-1610*, Southampton, 1920, p.30)

APRIL 8TH

1936: On this day, the Red Funnel paddle steamer *Gracie Fields* was launched by her namesake, who sang one of her most famous songs, 'Sing as we Go'. The locally built boat was destined to become a popular sight in her role as an Isle of Wight ferry.

In 1939 she was requisitioned by the navy for minesweeping duties, but when the evacuation of Dunkirk began she joined the fleet of 'little ships' crossing the Channel to rescue the troops from the beaches. She managed one successful crossing and returned the following day, 28 May 1940. Having loaded 750 troops, she started the return journey – but was hit by a shell. However, HMS *Pangbourne* came to her aid. After taking all the soldiers off the *Gracie*, *Pangbourne* tried to tow her back, but the steamer's rudder was stuck and she was taking on water, so had to be abandoned. She sank in the Channel two days later. J.B. Priestley referred to her in a broadcast: 'She has paddles and churns away for ever. But now look – this little steamer, like her brave and battered sisters, is immortal. She'll go sailing proudly down the years in the epic of Dunkirk...' (Various shipping websites; A. Rance, *Southampton: An Illustrated History*, Southampton, 1986)

APRIL 9TH

1917: On this day, Basil George Mitchell was born.

Basil attended King Edward VI Grammar School in Southampton and went on to Queen's College, Oxford. During the Second World War, he served in the Royal Navy and then took up an appointment as tutor in philosophy at Keble College, Oxford. He always regarded himself as a philosopher who was also a Christian, and never claimed to be a theologian. However, he did succeed in uniting the Theology and Philosophy departments at Oxford to create a new undergraduate course in combined Philosophy and Theology. Mitchell believed that there should always be a place for religious belief in public debate, even within a secular society. He argued that ultimately, even liberal humanism would have to consider the morality of its actions within a society. His approach to moral issues involved him in a number of working parties, studying ethical problems arising from scientific and medical research. Many thorny issues were examined, such as medical care for the dying, euthanasia and abortion. After such discussions, he returned home to the gentler pursuits of gardening and flower arranging. (The *Telegraph* obituaries, 14 July 2011)

APRIL 10TH

1912: On this day, the White Star Line ship *Titanic* sailed from Southampton on her maiden voyage. The most luxurious liner yet built, she was hailed as a great engineering achievement, with her new-style turbine engines and watertight compartments.

She sailed for New York via Cherbourg and Queenstown, where she had taken on most of the emigrant passengers. Midway across the Atlantic, travelling at approximately twenty-three knots, she struck an iceberg and, breaking in two, sank with the loss of 1,500 people. The 705 survivors were rescued by the Cunard liner *Carpathia*. The loss was keenly felt in Southampton, which had provided the ship with many crewmembers in the engineering and victualling departments. These two sections suffered the highest casualties, as they were not classified as 'seamen' and therefore could not officially be used as lifeboat crew. More than 500 Southampton families were affected and the whole town was plunged into mourning. Passengers on board the returning *Olympic*, *Titanic*'s sister ship, made a collection for the victims' families. When she docked at Southampton the money was given to the Mayor and was the beginning of the Titanic Fund, which would sustain many of the victims' families for years to come. (J. Eaton and C. Haas, *Titanic: Triumph and Tragedy*, Yeovil, 1995)

APRIL 11TH

1445: On this day King Henry VI's bride-to-be, Margaret of Anjou, was safely lodged at God's House.

At this time Southampton's relationship with the Crown was good, and one of its leading citizens, William Soper, had been asked to meet the future Queen at Rouen and bring her safely to England. They had landed at Portsmouth on 9 April, where Margaret had rested before continuing to Southampton by water. She then remained at God's House for four days, reputedly busy with the royal dressmaker who had come down from London. On 14 April she was conducted to the castle for her rendezvous with the King, and eight days later they were married by the Bishop of Salisbury at Titchfield Abbey. Within a few years, England was embroiled in the Wars of the Roses. After a series of setbacks, Margaret went to France seeking support for Henry VI. She returned to England on 14 April 1471 via Southampton. In May, at Tewkesbury, Margaret led her troops into battle for the last time. The battle resulted in the death of her son (the Prince of Wales), the murder of her husband and the imprisonment of herself. (J.S. Davies, *A History of Southampton*, Southampton, 1883, p.471; C. Platt, *Medieval Southampton*, 1973, pp.137-8, 149)

APRIL 12TH

1482: On this day, John Spryngge brought a complaint against Luke de Lago and Paul Stephan for causing the death of his horse.

Spryngge claimed that the pair had chased his horse – which was at pasture, supposedly on one of the areas of common land in the town – and deliberately threw it into one of the town ditches. The fall killed the animal. His story, however, seems to come unravelled when he says that the horse was chained to another one, which also fell into the ditch. It therefore seems more likely that the animals were not at pasture at all, but harnessed to a cart or something else. So how did they fall into the ditch? Probably this is an example of a road traffic accident, with one driver going too fast and the other either not willing or not able to give way. Result? One pair of horses was forced into the ditch, killing one of them. Spryngge claimed damages of 33s 4d and the jury agreed, sending the defendants to prison until the debt was paid. (T. Olding, *The Common and Piepowder Courts of Southampton, 1426-1483*, Southampton, 2011, Part I, p.145)

APRIL 13TH

1774: On this day, James Crabb was born at Wilton in Wiltshire.

He was destined to become an itinerant Wesleyan preacher, and ultimately moved to Southampton. Here he worked among the neglected and poor members of the community, setting up a Sunday school in Kingsland (described as one of the most depraved areas of Southampton), preaching to the dockyard and railway navvies, and regularly preaching to the Itchen Ferry villagers, sailors and fishermen, who were described as 'a wicked clan wholly destitute of all spiritual instruction'. It was, however, Crabb's work with the gypsies which brought him to public notice. Moved by the treatment they received in court, he resolved to understand their customs and culture better. He visited their camps and invited them home; he undertook the education of some gypsy children and wrote books to bring their culture to others. His fame among the gypsy community grew, and he held an annual festival in fields near his home, which gypsies and local gentry both attended. Ill-health forced Crabb to end his activities, with the last meeting being held in December 1848, when he gave his farewell address to the gypsies. When he was buried in Southampton Old Cemetery in 1851, the gypsy community gave a large donation for his memorial. (Dictionary of National Biography online; Friends of Southampton Old Cemetery Newsletter, November 2007)

APRIL 14TH

1864: On this day Abraham Lincoln, the President of the USA, was shot at the theatre by the actor J. Wilkes Booth whilst watching *Our American Cousin*. The play starred Edward Sothern, from Southampton, as Lord Dundreary.

Wilkes Booth escaped from the theatre, but was injured and sought medical help. Dr Samuel Mudd took him in and gave him shelter, medical help and money before taking him to the neighbouring town of Bryanstown. During the search for Wilkes Booth by the federal troops, Mudd denied all knowledge of him. Ultimately, Mudd was implicated and thrown into gaol, where he remained for four years, only being released after he had proved invaluable during an outbreak of yellow fever in the gaol. He never practised medicine again and it was not until 1979 that his descendants got his name cleared of the taint of conspiracy in a proclamation by President Jimmy Carter. The story is supposedly the origin of the expression 'his name is Mud(d)'.

When Edward Sothern was buried in Southampton, in 1881, a stranger attended the funeral. Edwin Wilkes Booth, brother to Lincoln's assassin, had come to pay his last respects to a fellow actor. (Friends of Southampton Old Cemetery Newsletter, March 2009)

APRIL 15TH

1608: On this day the Town Crier, John Hudson, was dismissed for helping the poor women raise a riot aboard a hoy.

The problem had been brought about by the dearth of corn and its high price, which continued to rise rapidly, putting it beyond the means of the local poor people, who were becoming unruly about the situation. When a London-bound hoy, with a full cargo of grain, was moored in the channel off the Town Quay, the Corporation became concerned that a riot would develop. They therefore decided the hoy should be boarded, its sails removed, and the corn brought ashore and stored in a vault, for safety. A ruling that could, perhaps, be interpreted as piracy by the owners of the ship. The expected riot happened, led by the women of the town. Using the many small boats from along the shore, the rioters boarded the hoy. John Hudson was seen as one of the principal agitators 'that had animated the women in their disorderly rising about the corn and did carry some of them upon his shoulders into the boat to go aboard the hoy'. (J. Horrocks, *Assembly Books of Southampton, Vol. I, 1602-1608*, Southampton, 1917)

APRIL 16TH

1611: On this day, serious complaints were brought against John Hudson, the Town Crier. He had been slacking in his duties for maintaining the cleanliness of the Watergate and West Quay, as well as several other areas of the town which 'now do lie most filthy and foul'. This was nothing compared to his careless use of the town's keys. The jury recorded that:

> … we have received many complaints against him and amongst the rest that he having the keeping of the key of the Watergate doth at his pleasure let in and out peoples in the night time whereby the King's Majesty may be defrauded of his customs and other pillfryes [thefts or pilfering] may be committed aboard barques and ships, we think him not a fit man to keep any of the keys.

The Watergate was the exit from the public Town Quay, adjacent to the customs house, so cargo should have been unloaded and brought through the Watergate to the customs house, where the taxes would be paid. Although the complaint refers to loss of the King's revenue from customs, it's more likely the town was concerned with its own loss of revenue. However, they had supposedly fired John Hudson exactly three years ago! (*See* April 15th) (F. Hearnshaw, *Court Leet Records, Vol. I*, Part III, Southampton, 1907)

APRIL 17TH

1886: On this day, it was reported that Princess Beatrice's birthday had been celebrated in the town by flying the Royal Standard at the Guildhall (Bargate) and on other municipal buildings, while many shops and ships had flown flags as well.

———— ◆ ————

1886: On this same day, after a suggestion by Mr T.W. Shore from the Hampshire Field Club, workmen were now clearing rubbish from the floor of an ancient vault on the Western Esplanade. (*Hampshire Advertiser*, 17 April 1886)

APRIL 18TH

1874: On this day the body of David Livingstone, the explorer, arrived in Southampton en route to Westminster Abbey.

The *Malwa*, the ship bringing his body home from Africa, was delayed two days due to storms. Nonetheless, Southampton was prepared to give Livingstone's remains a suitably ceremonial, but dignified, return to Britain. The coffin was transferred from the *Malwa* to the Royal Pier, on board an Isle of Wight ferry. Two wreaths were put on the coffin before it was placed in a horse-drawn hearse. The Mayor, Mr Edwin Jones, and the Corporation headed the procession. As well as Livingstone's family and Henry Stanley (who had found the lost Livingstone and famously greeted him, 'Dr Livingstone, I presume'), there were representatives from the Royal Geographical Society, the churches, the Medical Society and Royal Naval Reserve. A band played the 'Dead March' from Saul and muffled church bells tolled; flags were at half-mast, shops shuttered, curtains closed, and many people wore mourning of some description, while others were very emotional. The procession made its way through the town to the railway station, where the coffin was placed in a special carriage for its journey to London. All newspapers reported that the reception was most imposing and suitable for the occasion. (J. Lewis, 'David Livingstone's remains', M. Taylor (ed.), *Southampton: Gateway to the British Empire*, London, 2007)

APRIL 19TH

1850: On this day, Edward Gregory was born in Southampton. When he left school at fifteen he joined the drawing office of the P&O Steamship Co., but, showing a talent for drawing and painting, he changed course and turned to an artistic career. He studied at the Royal Academy and was employed to work on the Victoria & Albert Museum decorations. His painting, *Boulter's Lock*, was described as a 'three volume novel in art, the guidebook and encyclopaedia of the manners and customs of the English people'. (Dictionary of National Biography online)

———◆———

1851: On this day, the magistrates fined James King and William Dibden 10s each for furiously driving their horses along the Millbrook Road. At the same session, Charles Payne was fined 40s for indecently exposing himself. (*Hampshire Telegraph & Sussex Chronicle*, 19 April 1851, Issue 2689)

APRIL 20TH

1619: On this day the Court Leet was almost overwhelmed with complaints about livestock in the town. Six butchers were fined for killing animals in their backyards – which was an annoyance to their neighbours – and twenty people were fined for having pigsties in the town. These were very smelly (and probably noisy); the pigs escaped into the town and it was a general nuisance to everyone.

Two animals which didn't cause any problems were the lions at the Bargate. At this time they were carved out of wood, and a presentment was made for them to be 'new varnisshed to preserve them from Rottinge'. These were matched by a pair outside Watergate at the bottom of the town near the Town Quay. (*See* April 7th) (F. Hearnshaw, *Court Leet Records, Vol. I*, Part III, 1907, pp.553-4, 557-8, 563)

APRIL 21ST

1551: On this day Thomas Krupe of All Saints was indicted for using the local well as a jakes (latrine). Moreover, he had been encouraged to do so by his landlady, Alice Bencraft, to deliberately annoy his neighbours. She was as much to blame as he was and the whole neighbourhood was complaining about her. The pair were ordered to clean the wells by midsummer or face a heavy fine.

The Bencrafts seem to have been a rather insubordinate couple. Hugh Bencraft was a town porter and the ringleader of their 'evil habits'. Porters were supposed to load and carry goods for their customers, but often they spent time in the ale houses, leaving the carriers to load the carts themselves. The porters then charged for work they had not done or used force against the carriers to get money from them instead; at the very least, the porters were overcharging their customers. It seems that 'neighbours from hell' are nothing new. (F. Hearnshaw, *Court Leet Records, Vol. I*, Part I, 1905, pp.29-30)

APRIL 22ND

1914: On this day, the memorial to the *Titanic* engineers was unveiled.

It is the biggest and best-known of the town's memorials to the crew who died on the ill-fated liner, and the unveiling was estimated to have been attended by 100,000 people. Dedicated to the memory of the engineers who remained at their posts to keep the lights of the ship burning until the very end, the memorial was originally paid for by public subscriptions and attracted donations from around the world. It was designed and built by Whitehead & Sons of the Imperial Works, Kennington Oval, in London and was originally unveiled by Sir Archibald Denny, president of the Institute of the Marine Engineers. As well as recording the engineers' names, the memorial also records Thomas Andrews, shipbuilder and managing director of Harland & Wolff in Belfast, who was in charge of the plans for the *Titanic*. The memorial, officially a Grade II listed building, has deteriorated over the years; weather and pollution have dulled the bronze panels and the figure of the angel standing on the bow of a ship. It underwent restoration and was unveiled, back to its former glory, in September 2010. (BBC news online sites)

APRIL 23RD

1605: On this day the Court Leet jury was reminded that the town was still in need of a new prison. The matter was outstanding from the previous year's presentments, even though it was required by law for the town to have a prison.

It had been requested that the new gaol be built in St Michael's parish, or some other convenient place within the town. This would be an additional gaol. The Bargate Gaol was the Common Gaol, used for felons and notorious malefactors. It was therefore necessary to have a different prison in another place, 'made for men of better quality'. It is not clear if this meant well-to-do criminals, or those who had committed high-class crimes. Eventually the new prison was made in St Michael's Square, adjacent to, and facing, the church, but there seems to have been little difference between these prisoners and those at the Bargate. (F. Hearnshaw, *Court Leet Records*, Southampton, 1907, pp.403, 423)

APRIL 24TH

1908: On this day the town was brought to a standstill by 2ft of snow, which had fallen between daybreak and breakfast time; hardly an accurate timespan, but it does give some impression of the speed at which the very large flakes of snow fell.

Afterwards the town was transformed into a 'fairyland'. Nothing comparable had happened since the 1880s, but this far exceeded those reports. Nationally there had been some snowfalls, but also bitterly cold north-east winds for some weeks, together with hard frosts. There was considerable concern for the crops, especially the orchards and the grass that would support livestock through the summer. The docks were at a standstill, and in the town the winds had caused drifting in places and the trams found themselves stuck – not only due to the snow on their tracks, but also the weight of it on their roofs and even balanced along their trolley arms. (*Southern Daily Echo*, 24 April 1908)

APRIL 25TH

1482: On this day, Robert Colman brought a charge of burglary against William Wastell.

The charge was that Wastell had broken into Colman's house and stolen a number of items. These included a mazer (large maple-wood bowl) decorated with silver, valued at 26s 8d; three silver spoons worth 10s; a bow and five arrows priced 2s; two cheeses worth 8d; a linen apron costing 8d; and a small piece of tanned leather worth 6d. He then did other 'enormities … to the grave loss of the said Robert' to damages of 100s (£5). This sounds as if Wastell vandalised Colman's home.

Wastell came to court and admitted everything Colman had charged him with, except the theft of the mazer. For that one item he was tried by a jury, found guilty and sent to prison. Mazers seem to have been popular items for theft that summer – another was stolen on 4 May, and a third theft was reported on 19 July when another silver decorated mazer was stolen. It is tempting to wonder if it was actually the same bowl being stolen 'to order', but we will never know. (T. Olding, *The Common and Piepowder Courts of Southampton, 1426-1483*, Southampton, 2011, Part I, pp.148, 157; Part II, p.325)

APRIL 26TH

1662: On this day, Samuel Pepys came to dine with William Stanley, the Mayor. Pepys was on Admiralty business, travelling along the south coast checking naval accounts. Staying at Portsmouth, he rode to Southampton via the 'short route', which meant he used the Gosport, Warsash and Itchen Ferries. On the way, he passed the Earl of Southampton's estate at Titchfield, which he assessed as being worth £6,000 per annum. He also noted a small churchyard where the graves were sown with sage. In some areas it was the custom to strew graves with herbs for a year, after which a gravestone was erected by those families who could afford it.

The Mayor entertained his guests with sturgeon, which had been caught locally the previous week. He told them that this was a very rare occurrence, not having happened for twenty years. Pepys did not think much of the caviare from the fish, because the seeds of the roe were not 'broke, but are all in berryes'. Riding around the town, he remarked that it was one 'gallant street and is walled around with stone'. Bevis's picture on the Bargate attracted his attention and he considered that 'the key [quay] was well worth seeing'. (Samuel Pepys Diary online; R.G. King, *Itchenferry Village*, 1981)

APRIL 27TH

1613: On this day, William Knitchen was fined 1s by Court Leet for allowing bowls to be played on Sundays. At the same time, nineteen people were fined for taking part in the illegal games.

Southampton folk had played bowls on God's House green since 1299, and over time this had become the town's official bowling green. The inhabitants had got used to playing whenever they wished, but, during the period of religious confusion after the Dissolution, the Corporation occasionally tried to enforce better observance of the Sabbath. This was usually associated with the need to raise some funds for the town's finances – a few quick fines for illegal Sunday activities could be quite lucrative. One of the court's concerns on this occasion was that Knitchen was lending the bowls to 'Common Bowlers espetially of meane qualitie'. However, it must be noted that, in 1587, two bowlers who were burgesses, and might be considered 'better qualitie', were involved in a brawl over a game, resulting in bloodshed. (F. Hearnshaw, *Court Leet Records, Vol. I*, Part III, p.456)

APRIL 28TH

1904: On this day the Cemetery Committee dealt with a troublesome problem in the graveyards. There were a number of complaints about flowers being stolen from the graves. They decided to engage an ex-policeman to patrol the grounds, and posters were placed around the area to advertise his presence and warning that theft of the flowers was a crime.

———◆———

1904: On this day the Royal Italian Circus performed at the Victoria Hall Skating Rink. This was an indoor performance, not under the canvas of a Big Top, and the huge building was filled to capacity, with a delighted audience. The performance was described as the only exhibition of its kind in the world and 'absolutely unique'. There was no mention of human performers; the display was apparently centred on the animals which were on show. The total number was estimated at well over 100 performing animals, including fifty monkeys, fifty dogs and thirty ponies, together with bears and goats. (*Southern Daily Echo*, 29 April 1904)

APRIL 29TH

1920: On this day Eric Rowland Moon, pioneer aviator, was killed in a flying boat accident at Felixstowe.

Moon had built his first aircraft, suitably called the Moonbeam, in the old Wool House in Southampton in 1910. In a letter to *Flight* magazine dated 11 June 1910, he described the machine as a 24ft-span monoplane weighing 260lb, with a 6ft propeller, using a JAP four-cylinder 20hp engine. He had already made several successful short flights at Blighmont Park, Regents Park and North Stoneham Farm (the future Southampton/Eastleigh Airport). His company, Moonbeams Ltd, produced motor launches and its marine engines were exported worldwide. Moon used his business travels to contact many leading British aviators and, at the outbreak of the First World War, joined the Royal Naval Air Service (RNAS), becoming Flight Commander when he was posted to East Africa. Here his bravery earned him the Distinguished Service Order and Bar, and the Legion of Honour. When he was shot down in January 1917, it was erroneously reported that he had been killed in action. In fact, he was a prisoner of war. After the war he became a squadron leader in the RAF and Commanding Officer of the Felixstowe Flying Boat station, where the fatal accident occurred. (Headstone in Old Cemetery; P.T. New, *The Solent Sky*, Southampton, 1976, pp.1-6)

APRIL 30TH

1948: On this day a swan, immediately nicknamed Sammy, landed on the railway line between the suburbs of St Denys and Bitterne.

A linesman, who saw the illegal landing, tried to encourage the winged visitor to go elsewhere. Sammy was having none of it and the linesman retreated to Bitterne station to consult the stationmaster. The official approach was that it was imperative to warn St Denys station, because a train was due shortly. However, it was impossible to contact the stationmaster there. Sammy had collided with the signal wire and put the bell out of action. With time growing short, the Bitterne stationmaster and a porter advanced down the railway line armed with brooms to chase the swan away. But instead, he advanced menacingly towards them! With the advancing Portsmouth train now in sight, Sammy finally saw the error of his ways. After a false start across the railway sleepers, a supreme effort saw him airborne – just in time. (*Southern Daily Echo*)

MAY 1ST

1976: On this day the Saints won the FA Cup at Wembley.

The final was considered a David and Goliath match, with Second Division Southampton the underdog against the favourites, First Division Manchester United. The teams used very different tactics. Manchester concentrated on a series of well-crafted passes using four, five or six players manoeuvring the ball from defence to attack. Southampton used long passes and clearances, with the resulting pressure imposed by Channon and Osgood. Manchester opened up more opportunities for goals but finished weakly, with the Saints goalkeeper only being really tested once. No goals were scored and extra time was looming when Stokes picked up a good pass and placed the ball in the top corner of the Manchester net. It was the eighty-third minute of play and Saints had gone 'marching in' to win the FA Cup. Incidentally, the Saints had been asked to defer to Manchester in the matter of the colour combination of their kit. Both teams wore red and white, which in an era before colour television made it difficult for viewers to distinguish between the teams. So, for the first time, Saints wore their blue and yellow strip. (FA Cup website)

MAY 2ND

1615: On this day at the Court Leet there were several presentments against people who had left refuse in the streets and gutters. Amongst the more offensive areas were the towers behind the walls, which the Court said:

> ... for the most part lie very beastly and filthy and are very odious especially in the Summer Season for all passers-by, we cannot learn the offenders, but for remedy do think it fitting they may be rather impalled [fenced round] and shut up rather than to lie open, for the better avoiding this foul and beastly enormity and the keeping them clean.

Thomas Lee, Matthew Craddock and Henry Lavender had not cleaned the ditches, while John Grant, William Earl, William Green and Thomas Mallsart all had noisome (stinking) gutters outside their houses. The West Quay was also littered up. Essay Whitiff had left timber scattered there while Edward Exton, an alderman, had left a boat on the quay. Few people took any notice of the fines and orders imposed, so the town continued in its malodorous state for another year. (F. Hearnshaw, *Court Leet Records, Vol. I*, Part III, p.477 onwards)

MAY 3RD

1483: On this day, Nicholas Fortune was mugged.

He made a 'complaint of trespass' against Hugh att Hall and Richard Edward; in other words, they had done him some sort of personal injury. This could include physical injury, or damage to property or business. He brought the complaint to the Piepowder Court, which meant it was heard almost immediately after the assault because this court was held most days. There was no doubt which sort of trespass Fortune meant. He claimed the two men had attacked him with swords, cudgels and knives, and taken 10s from him; he wanted his money back. Unfortunately, they did not admit the crime, so it had to go to a jury and would be a long, drawn-out business. Without any law enforcement officers apart from the night watchmen, law and order could only be kept by bringing cases to the local courts, which meant that people had to get the necessary evidence for themselves. (T. Olding, *The Common and Piepowder Courts of Southampton, 1426-1483*, Southampton, 2011, Part I, p.149)

MAY 4TH

1851: On this day the town was playing host to two foreign warships, the Turkish *Feiza Baari* (Glory to God) and the American frigate *St Lawrence*. The Turkish vessel was the first to visit England and its arrival caused a considerable stir in the town, especially the men's naval uniforms with the traditional red fez.

Both vessels had arrived at the invitation of the British government, to their respective countries, to provide items for the Great Exhibition in London. After the exhibits had been unloaded and sent to London by train, several days of banquets, presentations, gun salutes and visits between the Corporation and the two vessels took place. The warships had both brought a considerable number of high-ranking officials; the Turks also brought relatives of the Sultan. It was reported that, at the reception and meal provided by Mayor Richard Andrews, the Turkish visitors were quick to appreciate the many toasts offered, readily offering several of their own to their host, the Corporation and the American officers from the *St Lawrence*. The report concluded by saying that it became a very jovial occasion! (*Hampshire Advertiser & Salisbury Guardian*, 3 May 1851)

MAY 5TH

1620: On this day Stephen Chaplin, one of the town musicians, had his livery recalled and was dismissed due to his drunkenness and 'other mysdemeanours by him oftentimes committed'.

Apparently he had paid for his own livery and the town offered to reimburse him, but then thought better of it and reinstated him instead, on a promise of his future good behaviour. Chaplin had been appointed in 1613, in place of William Thompson, who seemed to have a problem with women! (J.C. Jeaffreson, *The Manuscripts of the Corporations of Southampton and King's Lynn*, 1887, p.28)

———— ◆ ————

1710: On this day the town was visited by four Indian chiefs of the Iroquois Nations. No explanation is given for the visit, but it was another good excuse for a celebration.

The guns in front of God's House and along the Platform were fired in salute, and the Audit House was illuminated. Usually such celebrations were followed with suitable conviviality, with the members of the Corporation consuming three, four or six dozen bottles of wine. On some occasions, hogsheads of claret were tipped into the town conduits for the enjoyment of the general public. (SCA SC2/1/9, 5 May 1710; A. Patterson, *A History of Southampton 1700-1914, Vol. I*, Southampton, 1966, p.21)

MAY 6TH

1641: On this day three Jersey sailors, John Blanpie, Phillip Brocke and Aron Guillam, gave evidence concerning the seizure of their ship by Barbary pirates.

The ship, the *Jonas* of Jersey, sailed from Southampton under charter to the Canary Islands. Nearing the Canaries they were attacked by a Turkish ship, and the *Jonas*, its contents and crew were taken to Algiers, where they remained in captivity. The pirates were not interested in the cargo; it was the crew they needed, as slaves. If any of the crew had useful skills for their captors, they could sometimes gain improved living conditions, but many finished up as galley slaves. The majority, however, would be put to work building the enormous palace for the schizophrenic Sultan Moulay Ismail – cutting and hauling stone, crushing stone to make the mortar, and strapped to carts like mules to shift the stones. The white slave trade had been going on since the mid-1500s and would continue for over 200 years. Sometimes the pirates would raid coastal villages in the south of England, taking men, women and children. Cornwall suffered great losses to this slave trade. During the 1700s, many escaped slaves managed to return to England via Itchenferry village. (R. Anderson, *Examinations and Depositions 1639-1644, Vol. IV*, Southampton, 1936, p.22; D. Vitkus (ed.), *Piracy, Slavery and Redemption*, Columbia University Press, 2001, *passim*)

MAY 7TH

1846: On this day, the new cemetery on the Common was consecrated by the Bishop of Winchester.

The situation in the limited churchyards associated with the town's parish churches had become intolerable. Before such decisions could be taken locally, requests had to be made to Parliament, asking that they pass a Bill allowing the town to obtain land for a new burial ground. The statistics quickly convinced Parliament of the need. The facts were straightforward: three churches had few or no burial facilities, two had very limited space, and St Mary's two-acre churchyard was coping for the whole town. St Mary's own population numbered 14,535, so the space was hardly sufficient for its own dead. The curate informed the Mayor that the churchyard was full and, with the summer approaching, burials could be very unpleasant. The new cemetery was completed in October 1845, with three separate chapels: Anglican, Catholic and Jewish. The last was discreetly placed near the main gate, with its own entrance, and obviously was not consecrated by the Bishop. Eventually this cemetery too became full, and the present Hollybrook Cemetery received its first inmate on 5 March 1913. (A. Patterson, *A History of Southampton 1700-1914, Vol. II*, Southampton, 1971, pp.54-5; A. Patterson, *A Selection from the Southampton Corporation Journals 1815-35, and Borough Council Minutes, 1835-47*, Southampton, 1965, p.154)

MAY 8TH

1803: On this day, two simultaneous sermons were preached on the death of Walter Taylor, who had died on 23 April 1803. One was given in the Anglican church of South Stoneham, and the other in the Above Bar Congregationalist church of Southampton, which he had attended.

Walter Taylor invented the circular saw and made pumps and pulley blocks for the Royal Navy. Both blocks and pumps were far more efficient than previous designs and improved the performance of fighting ships considerably. A philanthropist and fair-minded man, Taylor had built a private nonconformist chapel at his own home in Portswood Green, and also paid the Anglican vicar at South Stoneham parish church. One of his closest friends was John Newton, the reformed slaver turned abolitionist. This may have had some bearing on the presence of an African retainer in Taylor's household. Through his friendship with Newton, Taylor probably came into contact with Hannah More, founder of the Sunday school movement. Her ideas may have indirectly influenced him to establish a school for his workers' children at Portswood, where regular 'feasts' were also held for the children and their families. Such a feast is depicted in a painting by Taylor's daughter-in-law, Maria Spilsbury, held by Southampton Museum Service. (D. Lancaster, *Discourse Occasioned by the Death of the Late Walter Taylor Esq., of Portswood, Preached at South Stoneham Church on 8 May 1803*, Winchester, 1803; W. Kingsbury, *A Sermon Occasioned by the Lamented Death of Water Taylor Esq., of Portswood Green, Preached at Southampton May 8 1803*, Southampton, 1803)

MAY 9TH

1587: On this day a complaint about Peter Quoyte's dog was brought to the Court Leet by a group of townspeople, who had suffered from the dog's exploits. The proceedings record that:

> At the time of our sitting there has been a complaint made of [a] dog, between a mastiff and a mongrel, of Peter Quoyte's which hath strong qualities of himself, which going loose abroad, does many times offend the neighbours and will fetch out of their houses whole pieces of meat, such as loins of mutton and veal and suchlike, and a pasty of venison or a whole pound of candles at a time and will not spoil it by the way, but carry it whole to his master's house.

Quoyte was ordered to keep the dog tied up or pay a fine of 3*s* 4*d* every time the dog was found on the streets. Another person (perhaps the sheriff who presided over the court) has written wryly in the margin: 'a well qualitied dog'. (F. Hearnshaw, *Court Leet Records, Vol. I*, Part II, Southampton, 1906)

MAY 10TH

1639: On this day Jacob Thring, a fencer, was called to answer a charge of insulting behaviour.

He was charged with spreading malicious lies and rumours about Mr Gollop, one of the aldermen. Thring protested his innocence until William Higgins came forward as an eyewitness; Thring was put in the Bargate Gaol pending the next quarter sessions, where he would be tried for his behaviour. He admitted having made derisory comments about Mr Gollop, because Mr Gollop had met him in the street and called him 'Sirrah' and asked how often his (Gollop's) servant had attended Thring's school. The term Sirrah offended Thring and he clapped his hat back on his head 'and stucke it up before Mr Gollop'; the alderman then asked if he knew who he was talking to, to which Thring replied that he did not ride a gallop, but he knew that he spoke to Alderman Gallop. The description of the incident seems quite amusing, but insults were rated as crimes – especially when directed against local officials. It seems likely that there was some sort of sexual innuendo in the language and actions, which has disappeared over the centuries. (J.C. Jeaffreson, *The Manuscripts of the Corporations of Southampton and King's Lynn*, 1887, p.28)

MAY 11TH

1937: On this day, preparations were in the final stages for the celebration of King George VI's Coronation the next day.

National celebrations would extend over several weeks, including a fleet review in the Solent on 20 May. The town found itself at the forefront of the preparations, due to the number of important visitors arriving at the port before going on to London; it briefly hosted various foreign diplomats as well as celebrities of the time. The last rehearsals for the Southampton schoolchildren's massed physical training display at the stadium had taken place, together with rehearsals for a magnificent pageant which included Britannia and her attendants. The streets were well supplied with flags, streamers and bunting, stretching down the fronts of buildings and across the streets where there were no tramcar overhead cables. Flags flew from windows, shop windows were gaily lit, all the ships in the docks were 'dressed over all' and the town walls were to be floodlit. The festivities 'were linking the greatest and the least of society'. (*Southern Daily Echo*, 11 May 1937)

MAY 12TH

1579: On this day the Court Leet received a complaint against Widow Walker, on a suspicion of witchcraft.

No grounds were presented for the charge, but the court was asked to question her, and arrange for five or six honest matrons to see her stripped and search her body. They were to look for any 'bludie mark on her bodie, which is a comon token to know all witches'. This was the usual method of identifying a witch; supposedly it indicated the point(s) on her body where she suckled her familiar(s). Witches purportedly had various spirits that did their bidding; these assumed other material forms, usually an animal (cats and hares were favourites), which needed to be fed from the witch's body. An alternative mark was a third nipple, so any unusual wart could be sufficient grounds to condemn a woman. On this occasion the request to the court may not have been as sinister as it sounds, since it is also stated that the proof will serve 'either to stop the mouths of the people or else to proceed further'. It seems that Widow Walker was the victim of gossip and this was an attempt to clear her name. Unfortunately we do not know the outcome. (F. Hearnshaw, *Court Leet Records Vol. I*, Part II)

MAY 13TH

1228: On this day Nicholas of Shirley, Lord of the Manor, signed an agreement with the burgesses of Southampton, in Southampton Castle, giving up all claims to the common pasture lands, east of what is now Hill Lane.

This land would become the property of the burgesses and their heirs forever. In return, the burgesses agreed to drop the lawsuit against Nicholas, and made him a payment of ten marks. His tenants within the borough would have the same 'rights of common' over this land as the burgesses. The burgesses, however, would not have common rights on Nicholas' remaining common land, known as Shirley Common. By this agreement, the large area of land known as 'The Common' came to be one of Southampton's most valued amenities. Originally 'rights of common' meant the right to graze beasts, gather fuel (fallen wood, brushwood or turves), dig clay for bricks or pottery, and gather wild produce (like nuts, berries and edible fungi) and rushes (used to cover floors or make tapers for light). Now the Common is valued for its recreational and ecological value, with the Hawthorns Centre standing on the site of the old brickmaker's cottage, introducing visitors to the wildlife within the city. (*Southampton Common*, Southampton, 1979; C. Platt, *Medieval Southampton*, London, 1973)

MAY 14TH

1902: On this day, Southampton Borough Council Works Committee wanted to spend £850 on new horses.

This could only be achieved by making an application to the Local Government Board. Committee member, Captain Bayford, urged that this should be deferred for six months and the use of the combustion engine should be considered. He argued that now they had arrived at the days of motor cars and motor traction, they ought to adopt motor traction for the whole of their heavy work. 'The horse was a prancing, gobbling animal which ought to be relegated to the use of the huntsman and the horse soldier. The horse did not serve any useful purpose in commerce as compared with modern motors.' Unfortunately, the Mayor reminded the Committee that they had not had happy experiences with motors in the past. The recommendation of the Committee was adopted and they agreed to make an application to the Local Government Board, so remaining committed to horses. (*Southern Daily Echo*, 14 May 1902)

MAY 15TH

1576: On this day, Robert Crewe was fined for throwing a dead horse in one of the water pits on the Saltmarsh.

Understandably people were rather upset by the smell this caused in the area, and they were concerned that it was likely 'to breed Infectyve air'. This was an age when it was believed that the smells generated by rotting materials carried diseases, so a large rotting horse was certain to produce illness in anyone who breathed in the foul air emanating from the corpse. Crewe was ordered to bury the horse under the ground with 'convenient speed'. Possibly it was considered a suitable punishment if he fell sick afterwards. (F. Hearnshaw, *Court Leet Records, Vol. I, Part I*, 1905, p.137)

MAY 16TH

1868: On this day, Sir Herbert Walker was born in London.

Originally intended for a medical career, for financial reasons at seventeen he joined the London & North Western Railway. He loved it and quickly grasped the essentials of railway operation. In 1911 he transferred to the London & South Western Railway as their general manager, where he initiated a massive reorganisation and rebuilding programme at Waterloo, including the electrification of commuter routes. When LSWR became part of Southern Railway, Walker was the general manager and he put his plans into operation for Southampton, where the railway also ran the docks. The port was considerably enlarged, so attracting the ocean-going liners; at the same time, the line from London was increasingly electrified and the King George V Dry Dock opened in 1933. Southern Railway now had the largest electrified suburban system in the world. Walker encouraged cross-channel traffic as well, with the Golden Arrow as one of its train services. There was even an autocarrier, where forty cars were hoisted aboard from the quayside! It was his efforts which largely transformed Southampton as a port in the early twentieth century and, aptly, the road adjacent to the docks has been named after him. (Dictionary of National Biography online)

MAY 17TH

1603: On this day a request was made to the Court Leet that the cucking-stool should be replaced because the present one 'on the Towne ditches is all broken'. The complainants were concerned that there 'should be a new one forthwith to punish the manifold number of Scolding women that be in this Towne and other evil living women as hath been heretofore accustomed to be done'.

Although the use of a cucking or ducking stool was regarded as acceptable for scolds, the siting of the Southampton stool over the town ditches did not bode well for any woman subjected to punishment. The ditches were stagnant and full of rubbish, sewage and other filth. A ducking into the mixture would result in serious consequences for the woman's health. The following year, a refinement for the new stool was suggested – that it should have wheels so that it could be 'carried from door to door as the scolds shall inhabit so that they may receive punishment ... for their daily misdemeanours ... as is fitting for them ... [which] would be a great ease for Mr Mayor ... who is daily troubled with such brawls'. (F. Hearnshaw, *Court Leet Records, Vol. I*, Part III, Southampton, 1907)

MAY 18TH

1883: On this day, Richard Cockle Lucas died at his Southampton home.

Lucas was a sculptor, artist and eccentric, known locally for his statue of Isaac Watts facing the Civic Centre. At the age of twelve he had been apprenticed to a cutler and became proficient at carving knife handles. In 1824 he enrolled at the Royal Academy, where he regularly exhibited over the next thirty years. His particular expertise lay in small-scale wax and ivory carvings, especially portrait medallions, such as Dr Johnson at Lichfield. Many of these were exhibited at the Great Exhibition in 1851, subsequently being bought by museums and art galleries. Lucas's fascination with classical architecture prompted him to produce a series of models of the Parthenon and write various articles about it. The former excited much comment when exhibited at the British Museum. His dedication to Roman culture sometimes extended to dressing in Roman costume and driving a chariot down the Avenue, from his home at Chilworth. His wife, who Lucas appeared to regard as a fairy, had the singular pleasure of reading her own obituary (written by Lucas) printed, framed and hung in their dining room as a standard to which she should aspire. (Dictionary of National Biography online; Lucas's autobiography, held in Southampton Museums' collection)

MAY 19TH

1856: On this day, Queen Victoria laid the foundation stone of the Royal Victoria Hospital at Netley.

The hospital was erected as a direct result of the conditions which sick and wounded soldiers had suffered during the Crimean War. It was seen as a new symbol of national pride; a building of 'extent and beauty', said the *Hampshire Independent*. Extensive it certainly was, with a quarter-mile long corridor running its entire length. When used by the Americans after the Second World War, they reputedly drove jeeps along the corridor. When Queen Victoria arrived from Osborne House, on the Isle of Wight, the water was too rough for the tender from the royal yacht to tie-up at the specially constructed 300ft jetty, with its red carpet and evergreen archway awaiting the royal party. Instead, the tender beached on the shingle and its occupants stepped ashore amongst the throng of waiting people. Meanwhile, officials were hastily ripping up the red carpet and running to lay it on the beach. After this inauspicious beginning things went better. The Queen laid the foundation stone successfully. Placed underneath was a time capsule containing coins, Crimean and Victoria Cross medals, and papers signed by Victoria and Albert themselves. (P. Hoare, *Spike Island*, London, 2002)

May 20th

1631: On this day, John de Marine and Richard Hapgood were bound over for the theft of two tombstones.

Nicholas Pescod had been annoyed to discover that two of his Purbeck tombstones had been stolen. He knew exactly where they should have been – on the Watergate Quay near the great crane, with another tombstone belonging to him. They had been lying there for several years, until witnesses saw two being taken away by de Marine and Hapgood. The two men testified that they had taken the stones to Winchester, at the request of a stranger from Lymington. The stranger had told them that they were his and he was sending them to a mason in Winchester. Hapgood admitted that he had carried out the sale of the stones to the mason when they reached Winchester. De Marine and Hapgood were both sent for trial. What does seem extraordinary is that Pescod apparently felt it was safe to leave his property lying around for years, in a public place, and that he did not expect the tombstones to be stolen. Perhaps he trusted the townspeople; or perhaps he just trusted the death penalty that theft carried. (R. Anderson, *Examinations and Depositions 1622-1644, Vol. II*, Southampton, 1931, pp.90-2)

MAY 21ST

2011: On this day, the Hampshire constabulary stalked a white tiger at Hedge End, just outside Southampton.

They had received reports of the animal lurking in long grass near a recreation ground. The area was sealed off and police marksmen brought into the area. The local zoo was contacted for information on the best way to tranquilise the animal and the necessary darts were obtained. Luckily the tiger seemed to be enjoying a snooze and remained where it had first been seen. With all the preparations in place, a police helicopter took off with a marksman and the tranquiliser darts on board. As they flew over the area, the pilot reported that there was something strange happening: the heat-imaging camera, used to locate lost and/or unconscious victims, was not registering any heat from the area around the tiger. Going lower to investigate, the downdraft from the helicopter rotor blades dislodged the tiger from the grass and a life-sized cuddly toy blew across the recreation field. (*Hampshire Guardian*, 22 May 2011)

MAY 22ND

1483: On this day, Thomas Broune came to court because Frances Overfeld had tried to cure his bad eye, but had blinded him instead.

Thomas Broune told how he had had a disease called a 'pyn and webbe' in his right eye and had entrusted his care to Frances Overfeld, who was a doctor. Thomas had been assured of a cure and a price of 10s was agreed upon. He had already paid 16d towards the cost, but now he was seeking damages of £5 from Overfeld, who 'had poured so much infective dust into the eye of the said plaintiff [Thomas] that the said plaintiff had lost his eye'. Overfeld denied that he had caused the damage and the case was referred to a jury. The matter appears to have been resolved because, on 22 May, Thomas returned to court to report that his demand had been satisfied. Whilst the disease of 'pyn and webbe' may seem a strange complaint, the term is still in use. Pin and web is used to describe two different, but often related, eye complaints caused by exposure to dusty, windy conditions. (T. Olding, *The Common and Piepowder Courts of Southampton, 1426-1483*, Part I, Southampton, 2011, p.150)

MAY 23RD

1777: On this day William Wallis fell into a receiver (large vat) of scalding wort at Mr Hunt's brewhouse.

The principles of the brewing process have changed very little over the years; after the malt grains have been cracked by milling they are soaked to form a mash. The liquid from the mash is drained out into the receiver vats where it is boiled with the hops. This boiling is the important part of the process and lasts for at least an hour; not only would this have been important for ensuring the hops were properly blended but also, it would have sterilised the beer, making it safer to drink than the town water. This side effect would not have been understood in 1777, but beer probably tasted better than the frequently contaminated water. Poor William was a carpenter working in the brewery, probably carrying out repairs either to the building or the vats themselves. Aged seventy-four, he slipped and fell into the boiling wort. Not a nice way to go. (St Michael's parish burial registers)

MAY 24TH

1482: On this day John Clere was accused of trespass by Thomas Dymmock.

On the face of it, this is hardly a matter of any consequence. However, at this time 'trespass' could mean anything from breaking and entering to grievous bodily harm, i.e. trespassing on a person's body. John Clere was accused of entering Dymmock's house in Southampton 'by force of arms namely with swords and cudgels' and assaulting his servant. The assault was so vicious 'that her life was despaired of', but it didn't stop there. Clere 'then and there knew her carnally and did other enormities upon her'. A clear case of rape apparently, but it is not the servant woman who claims the damages of 40s, but her employer, for the damage done to him! It must be presumed that he felt aggrieved at the inconvenience caused by awaiting the recovery of a sick servant. John Clere came to court and admitted all the charges of 'the aforesaid trespass in manner and form which is brought and alleged against him … by the aforesaid Thomas'. There is one other fact of the case, which may have been relevant – the servant's name was given as Joan Whore. (T. Olding, *The Common and Piepowder Courts of Southampton, 1426-1483*, Part I, Southampton, 2011, pp.184-5)

MAY 25TH

1865: On this day, Mathilde Verne was born in Southampton.

Mathilde was the second child in what would be a family of ten children born to Bavarian parents, the Wurms. Her father John was the organist at St Joseph's Church, in Bugle Street, for thirty years. Her mother Sophie was a music teacher in the town. Perhaps not surprisingly, the four daughters were all musically gifted. Three remained in England and changed their name to Verne, but Marie made her career in Germany, retaining her original surname. Mathilde gained fame in London, toured the USA, taught at the Royal College of Music and became a regular performer at the Henry Wood Promenade Concerts. She trained her younger sister Adela and quickly realised that she was the better pianist. Mathilde began promoting Adela in Vienna, through her own connections with Paderewski. Returning to England, Mathilde and her sister Alice set up a private music school in London, where they gained a reputation for the quality of their student concerts; Mathilde claimed they had taught 1,400 pupils. Amongst these was Elizabeth Bowes-Lyon, who would become King George VI's consort. Mathilde gave her last performance at the launch of her autobiography and died the same evening, 4 June 1936. (Dictionary of National Biography online)

MAY 26TH

1937: On this day, 400 of the Basque refugee children were accepted by the Salvation Army in London.

Four thousand Basque children had arrived in Southampton, in the *Habana*, a few days previously and had been taken to the large camp set up for them at North Stoneham. Public sympathy and concern for the children had been aroused when news of the Spanish Civil War (1936-1939), prompted by the bombing of the Basque town of Guernica, had reached the outside world. Locally there were fundraising efforts to raise money for the evacuation vessel, *Habana*, and these efforts continued afterwards to support the children at the camp. Some were taken into care by various charitable organisations, like the Salvation Army. A few of the children were able to return home at the end of the Civil War, but the Second World War prevented others from returning and they ultimately remained in the countries that had taken them in. A plaque commemorating their arrival in Southampton can be seen by the outside entrance to the art gallery. (*Southern Daily Echo*, 26 May 1937)

MAY 27TH

1826: On this day the horse sales at Trinity Fair were reported as having been very poor.

There were more horses for sale than for many years; there were a few very valuable ones, an immense number of roadsters and saddle horses, and a good number of carthorses – but very few buyers at any price and most of the horses went back home again. The situation was much the same in the cattle sales. The fair was only enjoyed, it seems, because of the attractions of the pleasure fair, which was also livened up by a fight or two! (*Hampshire Telegraph & Sussex Chronicle*, 29 May 1826)

MAY 28TH

1912: On this day it was suggested that the Southampton Board of Trustees for the Titanic Fund should appoint a lady visitor for the dependants of the fund.

She would check on their health, especially the children, and ensure there were no irregularities in the use of the money allocated to each family. One recipient, Mrs Biggs, was found to have been spending her allowance on drink; her money was suspended for some weeks and only reinstated when another family member took responsibility for spending the allowance on her behalf. A Miss Newman was appointed to the post and became a familiar figure cycling around the town, with her Dalmatian dog by her side, visiting each family once or twice a month. Locally there were 182 widows, 352 children and 280 other dependants supported by the fund. Miss Newman cycled a lot of miles. When her bike was stolen, the local trustees bought her a new one costing £4 12s 6d. Her stolen bike was recovered a short while later, during dredging operations in the docks. (Friends of Southampton Old Cemetery Newsletter, May 2007)

MAY 29TH

Date unknown: On this day, the working men of Southampton and other towns in Hampshire rose early to gather cuttings of oak trees, with the oak-apple galls on them, to observe Royal Oak Day.

The cuttings were stuck into their hats, or pinned conspicuously on their clothing. They also hung larger pieces to the knockers on the front doors of the wealthy, who took them in to place in their houses. After breakfast the working men went round to these houses for beer, but if this was not forthcoming they shouted the following rhyme: 'Shig-shag, penny a rag, Bang his head in Cromwell's bag, All up in a bundle.' But fear often prevented them from repeating the verse to the people who were probably their employers. However, the younger boys chanted it to anyone without an oak apple or oak leaf, mocking him for his lack of loyalty. The custom was widespread, with variations; locally it was known as 'shick-shack' and those found not wearing an oak sprig before noon were likely to have a bucket of water thrown over them! The game ended at midday and if anyone was challenged later, the following verse was said: 'Shig-shag's gone past, You're the biggest fool at last.' And the challenger received the ill-treatment. (*Notes & Questions*, 1st Series, Vol. XII, p.100; D.H. Moutray Read, 'Hampshire Folklore', *Folklore 22:3*, 1911, pp.292-329)

MAY 30TH

1883: On this day there was a meeting of the Liberal Party at the Reform Hall, when the proposal for a Channel Tunnel was debated. The report considered that this was not the way to promote Southampton's best interests as a trading port.

— • ◆ • —

1883: On this day it was also reported that the Corporation, wearing their full regalia, had attended St Paul's Church in order to support its fundraising efforts for a new organ; an oil painting of Garibaldi had been accepted and would be displayed by the art gallery; a young child in Bevois Valley had died as a result of burns received when a bonfire set his clothing alight; and the Corporation advocated that its records should be printed and published as a means of promoting and recording the town's history. (*Hampshire Advertiser*, 30 May 1883)

MAY 31ST

1977: On this day, Mrs Edith Park was the first member of the public to walk across the new Itchen Bridge.

The long-awaited link between the east and west banks of the River Itchen had at last been built. It had cost £12m and, before its official naming ceremony by Princess Alexandra on 13 July 1977, the public were allowed to walk on it to enjoy the views without the noise of traffic. The official times were set between 2 p.m. and 4 p.m. Crowds gathered at the city side on the west bank and at Woolston on the east bank. Mrs Park had been determined to be amongst the first, and had arrived on the Woolston side at 10 a.m. By 1.30 p.m. she was getting rather cold and the foreman took pity on her and let her go across on her own. The *Southern Daily Echo* recorded the event thus: 'While hundreds of people waited for the starter's signal allowing them to walk over the Itchen Bridge yesterday afternoon, a little old lady beat them all by sauntering across on her own.' (B. Adams (ed.), *The Missing Link*, Southampton, 1977, pp.115-16)

JUNE 1ST

1839: On this day it was recorded that a further 20 miles of railway track between Southampton and London would shortly be opened, leaving only another 18 miles to be completed. This would mean that passengers could make their journey between the two centres in five hours, and had a choice of two classes of travel costing either 12s return or £1 return. (*Ipswich Journal*)

———————•◆•———————

1951: On this day, the *Southern Daily Echo* considered the difficulties faced by married couples when both partners worked, using the example of a long-distance lorry driver married to a snake-charmer. Problems arose when the wife fell sick and was admitted to hospital, leaving her husband to care for two large pythons. One was dispatched to the local zoo, but the second was tucked up snugly in the cab of the lorry. This python only needed a non-stop supply of hot-water bottles to keep it happy. (*Southern Daily Echo*)

JUNE 2ND

1609: On this day Thomas Crump, one of the town porters, was placed in the green stocks in the High Street.

The local authorities were hoping this would bring him to his senses. They had fined him for 'drinking inordinately' at John Jourdain's house, on a Sunday afternoon, only two weeks before and warned him that it would be the stocks next time. Therefore, when he was discovered 'starke druncke by eight of the clock this morning' on 2 June, it was a serious matter. To make matters worse, his fellow porters were complaining about his neglect of duty and, more importantly, the merchants' businesses were being hindered. The porters fulfilled an important duty carrying the merchants' goods to and from their premises, as well as between merchants after various transactions. For these men, time was money and delays could be costly. Their complaints against poor Thomas would have been taken very seriously. In early November Thomas was told that he must reform, otherwise his position would be given to Hutchins. He was called back again a week later and threatened with expulsion and punishment. No more is heard about Thomas Crump, so perhaps he did eventually reform. (J. Horrocks, *Assembly Books of Southampton, Vol. II*, Southampton, 1920)

JUNE 3RD

1614: On this day a sturgeon was caught by a local fisherman.

Sturgeon were classed as royal fish and were therefore supposed to be given up to the appropriate town officials. On this occasion it was presented to the Mayor – not only in his civic capacity, but also as Admiral of the Port. No record is available of any payment to Hollyhock, the Itchen fisherman (possibly from Itchenferry village) who caught the fish, but it seems unlikely that he would have relinquished it readily unless he had expected some sort of reward. However, it was William Wells, the water sergeant, who brought it to the Mayor, so maybe poor Hollyhock had no option but to give the fish up. Living on the east bank of the river, Itchenferry village people were outside the boundary of Southampton, although they were still within the parish of St Mary's. This unusual arrangement meant that they were not subject to the civic rules of the town. Once on the water, however, they came under the Admiralty Court rules, therefore would be obliged to surrender fish to the Admiral of the Port, i.e. the Mayor. (J. Horrocks, *Assembly Books of Southampton, Vol. III, 1611-1614*, Southampton, 1924, p.87)

JUNE 4TH

1992: On this day, an astrologist predicted that Southampton would have a new skating rink and the city's parking problems would be solved, because 'it was written in the stars'.

This good fortune had been started by the unusual event of two solar eclipses within a few days of one another. Moreover, these had taken place in Gemini, which was the sister sign of Southampton. The city itself is ruled by the sign of Pisces (but all Sotonians are aware of this fact, of course), which made the solar event in its sister 'house' extremely significant. Altogether the auguries for the city were very favourable and June promised to be a 'very special month'. (*Southern Daily Echo*, 4 June 1992)

JUNE 5TH

1944: On this day, the D-Day invasion fleet assembled off the Isle of Wight, ready to depart for the Normandy beaches the following morning. Ships came from Portland and Portsmouth, as well as Southampton itself.

Southampton had been the centre of Operation Overlord planning since 1942. A trial exercise in 1943 showed the port and its hinterland could contain 44,000 troops, which could be embarked at a rate of 11,000 per tide. The build-up of landing craft and personnel had begun in October 1943; twenty-four berths were allocated to the force, while hotels and public buildings became headquarters for different sections of the military command, both American and British. At the same time, the docks and construction companies were making various sections of the Mulberry harbour. This was the floating harbour and roadway, which would enable supplies and ships to reach the invasion forces in the days and weeks following D-Day. It would be towed across the Channel in sections and assembled off the beaches, providing moorings for ships and loading and unloading facilities. One unforeseen problem for the town was a shortage of beer for the vast naval and military population. Furthermore, glasses were scarce – jam jars were pressed into service instead. (A. Rance, *Southampton: An Illustrated History*, Southampton, 1986, pp.169-71)

JUNE 6TH

1839: On this day, the section of railway line between Southampton and Winchester was used for the first time.

The locomotive for this test run had been built by Summers, Groves and Day in their foundry, at the bottom of Foundry Lane (near the present Millbrook station). One of their locomotives, the *Jefferson*, was already at work in America on the Richmond, Fredericksburg & Potomac Railroad. The London–Southampton railway was intended to link the docks to the capital, but at this time only the Southampton–Winchester and London–Basingstoke sections were complete. When the entire route was finished, the company's name changed to the London & South Western Railway. On 10 June 1839, four days after the trial run, the inaugural journey took place, with a train comprising a locomotive, four carriages and a stage coach on a truck. The stage coach provided transport for the passengers for the missing section between Winchester and Basingstoke. Nothing changes, it seems! (A. Rance, *Southampton: An Illustrated History*, Southampton, 1980, pp.103-4)

JUNE 7TH

1920: On this day the yacht *Shamrock*, from Southampton, arrived at Ellis Island, New York.

The J-class yacht, which was owned and had been built for Sir Tommy Lipton, had arrived to act as a trial boat for *Shamrock IV* – his latest challenger for the America's Cup. Between 1899 and 1920 Lipton had built five challengers for the cup; all were named *Shamrock* and all were subsequently beaten. His efforts, however, made him one of the best-known yachtsmen of the Edwardian era. To crew a J-class racing yacht demanded the highest level of both sailing and technical skills. Such men were hard to find and highly sought after. Lipton found many of his crew from the village community of Itchenferry, situated on the eastern bank of the river, within the Southampton parish of St Mary's. It was here, in the Solent, that most of Lipton's crews were trained. Such was the expertise within certain local families that, on the *Shamrock*'s 7 June Atlantic crossing, no less than seven members of the twenty-two man crew, including the skipper, were members of one family, the Diapers. (Diaper Heritage Association website)

JUNE 8TH

1829: On this day the artist Sir John Everett Millais was born in Portland Street, and baptised in All Saints' Church the following December.

Millais became a prominent member of the Pre-Raphaelite Brotherhood; although some of his early paintings did cause considerable controversy, he went on to become one of the most successful and influential of the Victorian artists. He popularised the accurate representation of nature and natural objects. Paintings like *Ophelia*, *The Boyhood of Raleigh* and *Bubbles* caused him to be criticised for sentimentality, but they were popular with the general public and are still well-known today. Controversy followed his personal life as well, when he had an affair with – and eventually married – Effie, the wife of the poet John Ruskin. The couple felt the stigma of this for many years and, although they had become friendly with the Prince and Princess of Wales, it was only after a deathbed plea from Millais that Effie was eventually presented to Queen Victoria in 1896. (Dictionary of National Biography online)

JUNE 9TH

1992: On this day it was reported that the *Golden Hinde* was shortly expected to arrive in Southampton and stay for approximately two weeks.

Sadly this was not Drake's original flagship but a full-scale, seaworthy replica, and she had visited the port ten years previously. The reconstructed ship had been launched in Devon in 1973 and, like her namesake, had circumnavigated the globe since then and sailed many more miles than Drake's original ship ever did. On this occasion she had sailed from Northern Ireland to Southampton. When she arrived in port, her crew was expected to be in period costume and all the flags would be flying. Nowadays the *Golden Hinde* replica can be found in her berth at Southwark, London. (Golden Hinde website)

———— •◆• ————

1992: On this day it was also recorded that experiments were being carried out on cars that could run on natural gas and could be refuelled at home. (*Southern Daily Echo*)

June 10th

1913: On this day, in Southampton, Edward Penley Abraham was born. He would become one of the most important figures in medical research into antibiotics.

He grew up in the town and went to King Edward VI School, before going to Queen's College Oxford, where he graduated with a First Class Honours degree in Chemistry in 1935. After joining the Dunn School of Pathology, he found himself working with some of the legendary figures of medical and pathological research: Ernst Chain, Howard Florey and Sir Alexander Fleming. Their work became centred on developing synthetic varieties of penicillin, and other antibiotics derived from new chemicals, which would overcome the resistance that many bacteria develop against the original type of penicillin. Although widely acknowledged within the medical and chemical fraternities, Abraham's achievements are unknown to most people. Yet nearly all of us at some time in our lives have reason to be grateful for his meticulous and ground-breaking work on developing antibiotics. (Dictionary of National Biography online)

JUNE 11TH

1518: On this day, King Henry VIII visited the fleet of Venetian galleys in Southampton. Plague was rampant throughout the country at this time and the King requested that the crew were not present during his visit, as it had been reported that the galleys were infected with the disease. The Venetian Ambassador sent a report back to Venice, recording the successful visit.

After dining ashore, 'the King and whole court went on board the flag-galley which had been royally prepared with a spacious platform decorated with every sort of tapestry and silk'. The royal party was served with a variety of confections, including sponge cakes, before the evening's entertainment.

Then the officials of the galleys performed feats on slack ropes, suspended from the mast, this was to the great wonder of spectators unaccustomed to such feats. After this the King departed. Next day he had all the town guns fired again and again, marking their range, as he is very curious about such things. In the evening fireworks were let off.

(R. Brown (ed.), *Calendar of the State Papers*, Venetian Series, London, 1867, pp.445-6)

JUNE 12TH

1959: On this day a strange new engine noise was reported along Southampton Water. The SR.N1 prototype hovercraft was making its maiden flight.

The idea of a cushion of air supporting a vessel was not new. It had first been suggested in 1716 by a Swedish scientist, and was developed in 1915 by an Austrian one, but it was Sir Christopher Cockerell who made the breakthrough. In a classic piece of kitchen science, he mounted a small electrical fan above a coffee tin, with a cat-food tin inside it, producing a downward circular jet of air directed onto his kitchen scales. He found that the downward thrust was four times greater with the inner tin present. Here was the principle used by all the hovercraft ever produced. Cockerell patented the idea in December 1955. Commercial production went ahead at the Saunders-Roe factory on the Isle of Wight, and a hovercraft ferry service between Cowes and Southampton operated for many years. When the SR.N1 was first unveiled it caused considerable interest and the Duke of Edinburgh, in December 1959, persuaded Saunders-Roe to let him fly the craft. However, he went too fast and damaged the bow. This was never repaired and was affectionately referred to as the 'Royal Dent'. (Dictionary of National Biography online; *Southern Daily Echo*, 12 June 1959)

JUNE 13TH

1992: On this day, the *Southern Daily Echo* recalled the achievements of Hampshire athletes during earlier Olympic years.

Significant among these was Donna Murray (Hartley) from Southampton, who at seventeen was one of the youngest competitors at the ill-fated Munich Olympics in 1972. Donna had only moved up into senior athletics a short while previously and had had little international experience when she was selected for the Great Britain team. After the terrorist attack on the Olympic Village, which resulted in the death of eleven Israeli athletes, a memorial service was held in the Olympic Stadium. The International Olympic Committee was now faced with the choice to continue with the Games or cancel. They decided to continue, despite the shock and trauma that the competitors had all suffered. It is hardly surprising that the heart had gone out of the competition and Donna, like others, did not perform at her highest level. Nonetheless, she went on to become one of the best-known international sprinters in the world, winning two gold Commonwealth medals in 1978, various European medals, and taking part in three Olympic Games before retiring and turning to bodybuilding as an alternative career. (*Southern Daily Echo*, 13 June 1992)

JUNE 14TH

1822: On this day, permission was given to mark out a racecourse on the Common.

With the advent of fashionable visitors to the town in the eighteenth century, annual race meetings had been established on Shirley, Stoneham and Netley Commons. When Southampton declined in popularity, the race meetings had been discontinued; the nineteenth-century racecourse was an effort to reinstate them. The course was set up on the west side of the Avenue; its circuit can still be detected in the wide green tracks heading from the cemetery towards the boating lake. At the top of the course a grandstand was set up, lined in green baize. The races remained popular for about ten years and then declined again, making it difficult for the organisers to pay the expenses. After the 1848 meeting they were obliged to sell off the posts, rails and the materials of the stand. Another brief effort at reviving the races was not successful; the refined customers were no longer coming and the meetings became cause for alarm, due to the rowdyism, drunkenness and crime which had become associated with them. Quite literally a gamble that didn't pay off! (*Southampton Common*, Southampton, 1979, p.22)

JUNE 15TH

1794: On this day Richard Moresby was born, and exactly sixty years later he died on the same day. He was interred in Southampton Old Cemetery, on the Common.

Almost totally forgotten now, Moresby had been a distinguished captain in the Royal Navy. His expertise did not lie in sea battles, however, but as a hydrographer, maritime surveyor and draughtsman. Moresby charted some of the most dangerous waters in the world, providing detailed surveys and accurate maps for naval and merchant shipping. One of the most notorious regions was the Red Sea, with many vicious reefs which had wrecked ships of the East India Company because there were no reliable charts available. One of the two survey vessels hit reefs forty-two times. Moresby spent four years surveying the Red Sea – not only providing details on the reefs, harbours and suitable anchorages, but also where fuel, provisions and water could be obtained. After this survey was completed, he was sent to chart the islands and reefs that lay along the India to Cape trading route – charts and observation which were to be of significant use to the voyage of the *Beagle*, with Charles Darwin on board. (Friends of Southampton Old Cemetery Newsletter, November 2008)

JUNE 16TH

1290: On this day, Nicholas de Barbeflet of Shirley granted the fountain of Colwell to the friary, which was approximately 3 miles away.

The friars undertook to take the water from Colwell, in Hill Lane, underground to Achard's Bridge (Four Post Hill) and then to follow the highway down to the friary. Various 'relay points' were set up on the way; these were the conduit houses. One still exists opposite the Mayflower Theatre. Twenty years later, in 1310, the friars gave the townspeople access to the water, making the town one of the earliest to have its own piped water supply. In 1420, the friars were no longer able to maintain the pipework and transferred the rights to the water supply to the town, out of 'the particular affection which we bear to the Mayor and community of the town of Southampton'. Using a legacy from John Benet, the previous Mayor, all the pipes were replaced and new conduit houses were built. The locals fetched their water from the conduits and a supply was still maintained to the friary, via a system of stopcocks. (J.S. Davies, *A History of Southampton*, Southampton, 1883, pp.114-15; C. Platt, *Medieval Southampton*, 1973, p.144)

JUNE 17TH

1843: On this day Joseph Antony Swinburne was officially declared a lunatic, incapable of managing his considerable fortune.

He was a resident at Mrs Middleton's asylum (a nineteenth-century care home) at Nursling. She reported how he had deludedly believed that his second-floor room, without a fireplace, was turning his hair grey. She had moved him downstairs to a room with a fireplace, where he was much happier (and probably warmer). During the hearing, one of the important questions put to Joseph was whether he knew the price of a pair of gloves. The jury decided he was unable to manage his money, being incapable of paying everyday tradesmen like the butcher or baker. No account was taken that, being wealthy, he had no need to pay tradesmen personally. The ruling was made, therefore, that he was incapable of making a will. The jury decided he was a lunatic, and his wish to pass his affairs over to his second cousin was denied, apparently. No mention is made of who would be responsible for his fortune. The report leaves the reader with a feeling of unease about poor Joseph's future. (*Hampshire Advertiser & Salisbury Guardian*, Southampton edition)

JUNE 18TH

1624: On this day, Andrew Kinge from Kingston was eventually brought to justice.

Although calling himself a tailor, he had been involved in cattle rustling over a wide area and it was mainly due to the efforts of a determined servant, John Still, that Kinge was eventually facing the charges. John Still was the servant of a widow at Catherington, near Havant, and when one of her cows went missing he resolved to find it for her. He started by asking if people had seen the cow, and witnesses confirmed that it had been seen with Kinge. Through enquiries, Still found a man who was looking for cattle stolen from Wickham, and also found a man whom Kinge had asked to buy 'his' cows. Eventually, all the cows and Kinge were followed to Totton and then Southampton, where Kinge intended to sell the cows at the market. In an age before proper policing, and when anything like detective work was completely unknown, John Still's determination must be admired. He gathered an impressive selection of witnesses and produced a case that appears unassailable. Kinge was sent for trial. (R. Anderson, *Examinations and Depositions 1622-1644, Vol. I*, Southampton, 1929, p.39)

JUNE 19TH

1665: On this day, Colonel Walter Slingsby wrote that a house had been shut up on suspicion of plague. A week later he confirmed this with the news that eight houses were closed, and by 2 July plague booths were built on the town fields, ready to receive the sick. Four days later the town was isolated from others in the area.

The remaining officials, the Mayor and one Justice of the Peace, saw it as their duty to prevent the poor from breaking out and spreading the infection to the whole neighbourhood. The only priest remaining was Pierre Courand from the Huguenot Church, and he provided the spiritual needs for the remaining people. As was usual, the Corporation officials took charge of the goods of those dying from the plague, with the apparent exception of Roger Culliford's property. This was bundled up and locked in the room where he died, where it remained for four years. Ultimately, it was ordered to be secretly buried in his garden, unopened. The fear surrounding Culliford's possessions points to the belief that he had brought the sickness into the town from London. (M. South, 'An Investigation into the History of Disease in Southampton 1550-1800', unpublished dissertation, University of Portsmouth, 1983)

JUNE 20TH

1948: On this day the bells of St Mary's Church, inspiration for the famous song, rang out once more, after a silence of eight years.

The Second World War had reduced the number of church bells in the town, due to the loss of All Saints', Holy Rood and St Mary's churches. At the same time, St Michael's bells had been damaged and only its 'little bell' remained to chime across the ruined streets, when the ban on ringing church bells was lifted in 1943. St Michael's other bells were tested and used again at the end of 1944, but there were only eight, not the original ten bells. All Saints' bells were completely lost, but the melted metal from Holy Rood's bells was stored away and used to make the replacement bells for St Michael's; the complete peal rang out again in February 1948. Meanwhile, from the ruined shell of St Mary's Church a new tower and steeple rose up; the damaged bells had been recast and were rehung in the new steeple, above the shell of the building. On this day the renewed bells were consecrated and Southampton's Mother Church had a voice again. (E. Sandell, 'Song of the Bells', *Southampton Sketches*, Southampton, 1977)

JUNE 21ST

1593: On this day, a case of illegal bartering was tried by the Corporation. Amongst town officials who signed the hearing was Andrew Studley, who also signed John Jackson's name. Was this forgery?

Studley, an alderman of the town at this time, blatantly abused his position by taking food and goods from local traders 'by virtue of his authority and not paying for it'. When one of the traders' wives challenged him and spat at him in disgust, she was whipped for assaulting him. The Corporation could not believe her story. In 1603 they had to believe it, when the Deputy Steward, John Ireland, exposed Studley. When Ireland went to inspect the accounts after Studley's mayoralty, he found pages had been torn out and entries forged. When Ireland refused to be bribed, Studley tried to burn the books. Further investigation revealed that Studley had overseen a culture of bribery and corruption for years. He suffered the Corporation's severest penalty: loss of his burgess-ship and a heavy fine. He was allowed to remain as a free-trader in the town, but he lost his house and was almost destitute. (J. Horrocks, *Assembly Books of Southampton, Vol. I, 1602-1608*, Southampton, 1917, pp.28-30; T. James, *The Third Book of Remembrance of Southampton, 1514-1602, Vol. IV*, Southampton, 1979, p.13)

JUNE 22ND

1801: On this day a small boat belonging to Mr David Lance (a friend of Jane Austen) capsized while returning from Portsmouth.

The five occupants – four servants of the Lance family and the boatman – were caught in a sudden squall which overturned the boat in the main channel. Hanging on to the upturned boat, the four men and one woman tried hailing the Cowes packet about fifty yards away, but the master 'continued on his course, regardless of the cries of the unfortunate sufferers'. The report contrasts this with the action of Mr Langa, of Hythe, who put about his own boat, the *Mary* of Southampton, in order to rescue the victims. After they were taken aboard, 'every attention that humanity and feeling could require was shewn them'. In particular the report commends Mr Butter, one of the victims, for having supported the half-fainting female servant in the water, throughout their ordeal. No scruples about 'naming and shaming' here! (*Portsmouth Telegraph or Mottley's Naval and Military Journal*, Portsmouth, 22 June 1801, Issue 89)

JUNE 23RD

1609: On this day it was discovered that, the night before, a group of unknown drunken and disorderly persons had removed the green stocks from the side of Holy Rood Church and tied them to the Bullring.

The Bullring was situated in the upper part of High Street, where bull-baiting was practised not only as a form of entertainment but, as it was commonly believed, as a means of tenderising the meat when the beast was slaughtered. The night watchmen were considered to be obviously at fault and were questioned closely about the affair, but they all testified that they had neither seen nor heard anything. It was, however, felt that someone should be punished for the offence and Robert Webb, the principal watchman for the Bullring area, was sentenced to time in the stocks. It must be presumed that this was considered the best punishment to fit the crime. (J.W. Horrocks, *Assembly Books of Southampton, Vol. II*, Southampton, 1920)

JUNE 24TH

1994: On this Midsummer Day, a local public house celebrated Christmas.

This upside down state of affairs had originated three years before and had now become a local tradition, looked for by the regulars and others who came from farther afield. This was no English Christmas, but a full-blown Australian one with all the necessary trappings. A barbecue was set up in the back garden serving burgers, sausages and kangaroo steaks, while the Down Under Band provided the music – naturally this included 'Waltzing Matilda'. The owners had come up with the idea of sharing a taste of an Australian Christmas after returning from six years working 'down under' in the Australian hospitality business, at Alice Springs. While decorations, tinsel and fairy lights were in evidence, Father Christmas did not appear because, during their time in Australia, they had never seen that gentleman attend the festivities. (*Southern Daily Echo*)

JUNE 25TH

1999: On this day the Town Crier was called upon to be one of the judges in the Hampshire Best Beer competition.

This was a suitable choice as there had been a longstanding tradition that one of the Town Crier's duties was to assess the strength of the local beers; there were certain standards required for the strength of single beer and double beer produced by the beer brewers in the town. However, he would limit the assessment to taste only; the traditional method involving leather breeches would not be used. So how did the Town Crier assess the strength of the beers in the past? By putting on a pair of leather breeches, wetting a wooden stool with the beer, sitting on the wet stool and seeing how well the breeches stuck to the stool when he stood up! (*Southern Daily Echo*, 25 June 1999)

JUNE 26TH

1789: On this day King George III, Queen Charlotte and three of the princesses visited Southampton.

After receiving a loyal address at the Audit House, the party took refreshments before walking to the Town Quay to admire the view, which was considerably improved by high tide. With the King and gentlemen on horseback and the ladies in their carriages, they processed along the beach, before returning to Lyndhurst in the New Forest. The royal family were staying at Lyndhurst for a few days, breaking their journey to Weymouth. Part of their time would have been spent in the King's House, in Lyndhurst High Street, where the King and his family dined in one of the downstairs windows, so that 'people may see [him] at table'. As a result of a conversation during their Southampton visit, the royal party visited Alderman Ballard's Lyndhurst house, enjoying the fine views over the woods with the aid of telescopes. Afterwards, Mr Ballard renamed the house Mount Royal. The King had recovered from one of his bouts of sickness in February, and it is likely that this visit was to demonstrate his recovery to as many people as possible. (*World*, 2 July 1789; J.S. Davies, *A History of Southampton*, Southampton, 1883, p.503)

JUNE 27TH

1998: On this day the Southampton City Petanque Club was holding its annual competition at the Lordshill Recreation Centre.

The club had been formed twenty years earlier to enable local players and enthusiasts to take part in the World Championships, which were being held at Southampton Sports Centre that year. The 1998 competition coincided with this anniversary and promised to be an interesting event. About twenty teams of triples, drawn from clubs throughout the Southern Region of the British Petanque Association, would be competing over five rounds of matches for the Paul Slater Trophy. (*Southern Daily Echo*, 27 June 1998)

JUNE 28TH

1826: On this day a serious fire was reported at John Aslatt's coach-building works.

Nearly all of his uninsured stock was destroyed – which he may have felt was caused, in some measure, by the fire brigade. It was discovered that the hoses were in bad repair and the plugs so difficult to open that access to the water supply was delayed. Moreover, not all the firemen turned out; several were afterwards sacked for neglect of duty. Ten years later things were even worse! During the Chapel Fair, most of the thirty-six firemen seem to have been celebrating too well. A fire broke out at night and only fourteen or fifteen put in a very belated appearance, and of those only two were sober! (A. Patterson, *A History of Southampton 1700-1914, Vol. I, An Oligarchy in Decline*, Southampton, 1966, p.142)

JUNE 29TH

1994: On this day a courting couple allowed passion to get the better of them and to overwhelm discretion. In the heat of the night (and presumably the moment) they had to cool their ardour after being spotted outside a pub in the city centre by a police patrol, who told them to 'move along'.

———•◆•———

1994: On this day prisoners in Albany Gaol on the Isle of Wight, and their wives and children, were given a special meal. Albany housed some of the longest-serving 'lifers' in the country, and the authorities sanctioned the treat as a means of easing the difficulties suffered by the families, caused by their long separations. The meal was prepared by the gaol's own catering department. Unfortunately, the lunch caused considerable controversy and criticism when it was discovered that the menu had included caviare and quails' eggs! (*Southern Daily Echo*, 29 June 1994)

JUNE 30TH

1989: On this day the Sarah Siddons Fan Club performed their inaugural production, entitled *Taking the Flounce, or How Nelson Lost his Other Eye*.

The Fan Club is a street theatre group which comprises enthusiastic local historians; they are intent on popularising Southampton's rich history by introducing the public to characters and events linked to various venues within the town. This first production was led by Miss Jane Austen herself, who introduced audiences to the delights of the Southampton Spa. The company has developed its own idiosyncratic, but accurate, style of interpretation, with members researching their own historical characters for each production. Plays have been devised for and performed at Netley Abbey, Romsey, Tudor House and other venues. Subjects have ranged from the legend of Sir Bevis of Hampton (performed as a pantomime), *Titanic*, and the harrowing tale of the cannibalised Richard Parker. So where did the name come from? A joke! In 1989 the rising stars of the pop world were the Joan Collins Fan Club. The street theatre group had no name, so, when a reporter asked what they were called, the reply came back amending the pop group name to the Sarah Siddons Fan Club – and it stuck! (Sarah Siddons Fan Club archive)

JULY 1ST

1822: On this day, a race meeting was held on the Common.

This was an attempt to revive the town's flagging visitor trade by making the race meeting part of a week-long programme of events. These would include the opening of the theatre's season, special dinners at the Dolphin and Star, a ball at the Long Rooms, and a firework display at Houndwell for the amusement of the poorer folk. A new grandstand, tastefully lined with green baize, had been built at the north end of the racecourse as an additional attraction. The race-goers were able to avail themselves of a variety of refreshments, including raspberry vinegar and soda water, lemonade, sherry punch and genuine ale brewed at the Cowherd's Inn. Itinerant vendors provided ices and fruit. Sideshows included prize-fighting bouts, while Mr Punch amused the many travellers along the road. It was claimed that there were no horse-drawn vehicles available in the town on race days, because they were all hired out, often at exorbitant prices, to the hundreds of people going to the races. The revival was short-lived and, after the 1848 meeting, the materials from the stand, posts and rails had to be sold to cover the expenses. (A. Patterson, *A History of Southampton 1700-1914, Vol. I*, Southampton, 1966, pp.132-3; *Southampton Common*, Southampton, 1979, p.22)

July 2nd

1887: On this day the greenhouses at Wilton House, owned by Mr H. Buchan, were full of orchids in full bloom. An exceptional specimen of *Odontoglossum hallii* had a flower spike over 5ft long. (*Hampshire Advertiser*)

————◆◆————

1985: On this day it was reported that the cool wet summer had, so far, freshened the gardens and brought out bright-coloured displays of flowers everywhere; sure to cheer everybody up.

————◆◆————

1985: On this day it was also reported that local biologists were working to genetically engineer trout to make them resistant to the pollution in our rivers and enable them to grow larger. (*Southern Daily Echo*)

JULY 3RD

1612: On this day the town was given a copy of the 'new Bible' by John Favour.

This was, of course, the new version of the Bible which had been initiated by King James and had been published in May 1611. John Favour had been born in Holy Rood parish, Southampton, in January 1557, and by 1612 he was a lawyer and vicar of Halifax. He gave precise instructions about how, where and why the Bible should be kept in the town. It was to be chained to a desk in the Council Chamber of the Audit House, to be 'the edification of those who shall reade therein as also that by the sight thereof the good Magistrates may be put in mind of mercy and judgement and to doe all things to God's glorie and in love of their brethren'. The Bible was valued at 50s; this has to be viewed in comparison with the one bought for the school three months later, which cost just 12s. Favour's gift remained in the Council Chamber as he had requested, only being removed for rebinding in 1733. (J. Horrocks, *Assembly Books of Southampton, Vol. III, 1611-1614*, Southampton, 1924, p.44)

JULY 4TH

1940: On this day Jack Mantle gained the only Victoria Cross awarded to the navy for an act of valour on mainland Britain during the Second World War.

Twenty-three-year-old Jack lived in Southampton and had attended Taunton's School before joining the Royal Navy. He was serving on HMS *Foylebank* in Portland harbour when the ship came under heavy attack from enemy aircraft. The citation for his VC reads:

> Leading Seaman Jack Foreman Mantle was in charge of the starboard pom-pom [gun] when HMS *Foylebank* was attacked by enemy aircraft.
>
> Early in the action his left leg was shattered by a bomb, but he went on firing his gun, with hand gear only, for the ship's electric power had failed.
>
> He suffered several further wounds but his great courage bore him up until the end of the fight, when he fell by the gun he had so valiantly served.

He was buried at the Naval Cemetery at Portland, where his Commonwealth War Graves Commission headstone bears an engraving of the Victoria Cross, which was awarded to his family posthumously. After the war a small children's playground, Jack's Corner, was created at Southampton Sports Centre in his memory. (Naval Victoria Cross awards online; A. Rance, *Southampton: An Illustrated History*, Southampton, 1980, p.164)

JULY 5TH

1665: On this day the remaining members of the Corporation made a general plea for help during the outbreak of plague.

The sickness had been in the town for two weeks; law and order had broken down and they were facing starvation as well because the 'pestilential disease is still raging, putting an utter [end] to our traffic ... and affrighting the country [people] from bringing in their accustomed provisions [to the markets] we seem to be threatened with famine as well as pestilence ...' They asked the justices for a general tax to be levied in the adjacent areas to raise money to relieve their distress. The next day they sent another letter to Lord Ashley, Lord President of the council, asking for their case to be brought before the Lord Treasurer and requesting a surgeon or physician who would not be scared of treating the sick. The letters had the desired effect; the King gave notice that Southampton should receive provisions and a surgeon, while a special tax for the relief of all afflicted areas would be levied nationally. Southampton continued to be affected by the plague until December, and only then did people start to return to their homes. (J.S. Davies, *A History of Southampton*, Southampton, 1883, pp.498-9)

JULY 6TH

1522: On this day Emperor Charles V of Spain left England from Southampton, accompanied by 180 of his ships, including many of the Venetian galleys visiting the port.

The Emperor had stayed in the town for a week, after a long visit to King Henry VIII in London. Being the two most powerful Christian monarchs in Europe at this time, it had been hoped that they would combine forces against the Turks who, under Suleiman, appeared to be threatening Hungary and Bohemia; but the war never happened. Every royal visit meant celebrations, and elaborate displays to demonstrate loyalty and allegiance to the visitors. This visit was no exception and Charles entered Southampton through the decorated Bargate. This was probably when the two great painted wooden panels, showing Sir Bevis of Hampton and his squire Ascupart, were hung on each side of the gateway. Sir Bevis and Ascupart were characters from a twelfth-century romantic poem and were intended to recall the town's ancient traditions for the Imperial visitor. It is likely that the wooden forerunners of the present lions at the Bargate were also put in place for Charles's visit, since they are also part of the Bevis story. (A. Rance, *Southampton: An Illustrated History*, Southampton, 1980, p67; J.S. Davies, *A History of Southampton*, Southampton, 1883, p.478)

JULY 7TH

1637: On this day Widow Rouse was given permission, by the Assembly, to remove soil from the town ditches.

A large amount of people's filth was illegally thrown into the ditches, and the channels constantly needed clearing. 'Soil' was not a description of 'earth' in this context, but a rich mixture of dead animals, dung, offal, ordure and rotting vegetables. Widow Rouse appears to have wanted this foul mixture to spread on her own ground, presumably as a means of fertilising it and making it more productive. This use of human sewage and general refuse was a practical way of removing the problem, but the waste was also considered an asset which should be made available to the community. Widow Rouse was therefore directed to take every seventh load that she removed to the Saltmarsh for the use of the town. Here she should lay it in the five places 'as she shall be assigned'. How big a 'load' was, or how extensive her grounds were, must remain matters for speculation. (Assembly Books, SRO, SC 2/1/7, 1602-1642)

July 8th

1833: On this day the pier was named 'Royal Pier' by the Duchess of Kent and the young Princess Victoria.

The Duchess and her daughter were staying at Norris Castle, at East Cowes, and travelled from the Isle of Wight to Southampton in the royal yacht *Emerald*. They were met by a state barge, steered by Admiral Tinling, which carried a deputation representing the Corporation, gentry and merchants of the town. At the bow of the barge was the silver oar, the badge of Southampton's Admiralty over the waters. The deputation then invited the royal ladies to land at the foot of the pier steps, where they were met by the Mayor and Corporation. After taking refreshments in a marquee at the pier-head, the Duchess graciously accepted the invitation to name the pier, saying, 'It affords me great pleasure to name the pier the Royal Pier, and I add our sincere good wishes that it may promote the prosperity of the town.' It was estimated that approximately 25,000 people came to watch the ceremony. (J.S. Davies, *A History of Southampton*, Southampton, 1883, p.516)

JULY 9TH

1174: On this day, King Henry II landed at Southampton to begin his pilgrimage of atonement to Canterbury, after the murder of Thomas Becket.

Henry II and Becket had been good friends until the King appointed Becket as Archbishop of Canterbury. Tensions developed between them when Becket entered into his role with genuine religious fervour. Henry expected his new Archbishop to be his 'yes-man', but they disagreed violently about aspects of Church law and its relationship to criminal law. Things erupted during a meeting at Clarendon Palace and, after the King brought various false charges against him, Becket went into exile in France. Tempted back to England by a compromise, on arrival Becket immediately excommunicated his enemies. When Henry heard this, he flew into a rage and supposedly spoke the words, 'Will no one rid me of this troublesome priest?' Four knights took him at his word, rode to Canterbury Cathedral and murdered Becket. Overcome with remorse, Henry vowed to undertake a pilgrimage of penitence, which he began at Southampton. Where the King went, so others followed, and the route from Southampton via Winchester to Canterbury is still walked by modern pilgrims. (C. Platt, *Medieval Southampton*, 1973, p.13; http://www.bbc.co.uk/history/british/middle_ages/becket_01.shtml)

JULY 10TH

1711: On this day Henri Portal, a Huguenot refugee, became a naturalised British subject.

Originally part of the French nobility, the Portal family had been persecuted for their beliefs. According to tradition, when the chateau was raided Henri and his brother Guillaume were hidden in an oven by an old servant, before being smuggled out of France in wine casks on board a lugger bound for Southampton. Here they landed and joined the Huguenot community in the town. In 1710 Henri worked in a paper mill at South Stoneham, learning the trade that would make the family name famous. Here he met and was befriended by Sir William Heathcote, from Hursley. Two years later, Heathcote helped Henri to lease a mill at Whitchurch, where he founded the Portal paper-making empire; by 1718 he had a mill at Laverstoke too, and in 1724 he gained the contract to make the paper for Bank of England banknotes. The business was passed on, father to son, for nearly 250 years, and the banknote contract remained with the company until it was finally bought by De la Rue in 1995. (Hampshire Mills website)

JULY 11TH

1801: On this day Stephen Buckle returned to Southampton after being released from prison in France.

Buckle was a local ferryman and had been hired by three Frenchmen to take them to the Isle of Wight. When they were in the Solent, the three men jumped him and tied him up, threatening him with death unless he helped them reach France. Luckily the sea was calm and, after two days and nights rowing, they reached Cherbourg safely. All three Frenchmen were put in gaol because they were escaped prisoners. Buckle joined them, until a native of Southampton, living in Cherbourg, gained the boatman's release and restored his boat to him. He and his boat were returned to Southampton in a cartel vessel. The report makes it clear that the helpful Sotonian resident of Cherbourg had aided the release of many other English captives. Was this Southampton's own Scarlet Pimpernel? (*Mottley's Naval and Military Journal*, 18 July 1801)

July 12th

1952: On this day, a talk on the history of education in Southampton revealed some shortcomings in the school inspector scheme.

Until 1904, teachers had been paid by the results of these inspections. Reading skills were tested by the inspectors listening to a child read from a book that the pupils had chosen themselves. Often the pupils were coached and learnt the passage by heart without having to read it at all. Another useful trick took place when the teacher asked the class a question: children who were certain of the answer put up their right hands; those who were not, put up their left hands. (*Southern Daily Echo*)

JULY 13TH

1604: On this day, Anthony Antonie wrote to Captain Thomas Stockwell enquiring about the safety of the town during the outbreak of plague.

He had heard that it was very severe – enough to 'terrifie me from coming thither'. On 21 July, Antonie wrote again because he had heard nothing from Stockwell and was concerned that the disease had struck the latter's family. Stockwell obviously replied to this letter and the response from Antonie was swift; on 23 July he sent a long letter of sympathy, full of condolences for the loss of Stockwell's wife. He tried to comfort him with the fact that his two children had been spared. Antonie ended the letter by reassuring his friend that it would all work out for the best. The letter Stockwell received from his employer, Oliver Lambert, was much more prosaic: 'Tom, I am sorry for the loss of thy wife. Yet it is the way to be rich to have many wives. Look well before you leap and marry a rich one or none.' (J. Rutherford, *The Stockwell Letters 1590-1611, Vol. I*, Southampton, 1932, pp.22-6)

JULY 14TH

1609: On this day, Widow Cooper brought a claim for 40s against Denis Rowse.

She claimed that this was in recompense to her son, who had been dismembered (castrated) by a 'lunatic woman'. Widow Cooper's son had apparently paid the woman for some kind of medical treatment, but instead she had castrated him. He had since died, although no mention is made about this being linked to the wounding. How Denis Rowse came to be involved is not clear, but Cooper seemingly thought that Rowse was holding the cash in surety for the 'lunatic woman'. However, he swore on oath that he knew nothing of the money and had never received anything from anyone. Instead, it was poor Widow Cooper who found herself in the dock for trying to claim money under false pretences! Sounds like a case of rough justice. (J. Horrocks, *Assembly Books of Southampton, Vol. II, 1609-1610*, Southampton, 1920, p.46)

JULY 15TH

1951: On this day a series of fatal accidents were reported, which were apparently related to the sudden heat wave of the previous day, when temperatures had reached a record 30°C. An experienced swimmer had collapsed and died while bathing at Weston Shore, possibly due to the sudden shock of the cold water; a crash at Shirley had been so violent that the impact had caused one driver to be thrown out of the car door, whereupon he struck his head on the kerb and died instantly; and a lady so overcome with heat and thirst accidentally drank disinfectant and died. (*Southern Daily Echo*)

JULY 16TH

1945: On this day, John Arlott resigned from Southampton Police to join the BBC as Talks Producer for the Eastern region.

He had joined up, aged twenty, eleven years earlier on 31 August 1934. During his police service he had joined Special Branch, screening aliens entering the country during the war. In 1940 he married his first wife, Dawn Rees, a nurse, and they moved into Howard Road in Shirley. It was during this period that he began to write poetry, including *Clausentum* (a book of twelve sonnets) to complement Michael Ayrton's drawings of Bitterne Manor House, the site of the Roman settlement of Clausentum. It was through his poetry that he joined the BBC, having been recommended by John Betjeman. Within a short while, he was broadcasting in various features and talks programmes. In 1946 he was offered a chance opportunity to commentate on the Indian cricket tour to England that year. The next year he commentated on the South African tour and county cricket, quickly becoming an indispensable part of the team. His ability to observe small details, and his naturally poetic turn of phrase, painted pictures for the listeners which encapsulated the spirit of the game. Arlott had become the international 'voice of cricket'. (*Dictionary of National Biography*; Police Record of Service SC/P6/1/4)

July 17th

1674: On this day Isaac Watts, the hymn writer, was born.

The eldest child of nonconformist parents, Isaac began writing poetry – which he regarded as a divine gift – as a child. His gift came to the family's notice when they were at prayers one day; young Isaac was heard to titter and his father demanded to know the reason. Pointing to the bell-rope by the fireplace, he replied, 'Because I saw a mouse run up that and the thought came into my mind: "There was a mouse for want of stairs / Ran up a rope to say his prayers".' Watts wrote several influential books and poems before finally turning to hymn writing. He had complained about the quality of hymns sung at Southampton, and his father had told him to mend the matter, which he did very successfully. After this, his brother Enoch urged him to publish his hymns and psalms. These include: 'Jesus shall Reign Where'er the Sun'; 'When I Survey the Wondrous Cross' and 'Come Let us Join our Cheerful Songs'. His statue stands in Watts Park, facing Southampton's Civic Centre, where the clock chimes out his hymn, 'O God Our Help in Ages Past' every four hours. (D. Fountain, *Isaac Watts Remembered 1674-1748*, Worthing, 1974; Dictionary of National Biography online)

JULY 18TH

1891: On this day the Bitterne Cycle Club took their usual weekly ride, with thirteen members riding to Stoney Cross.

They left their headquarters at 3 p.m. and cycled to Rufus Stone; after this, some refreshment was called for, and they adjourned to the Sir John Barleycorn public house. Their host, Bradford, provided sustenance and also showed them an old settle where King Rufus and the Bishop of Winchester reputedly sat and played cards! With Miss Bradford 'presiding at the piano, the party were put into good spirits by the rendering of some capital harmony by Messrs Holdaway, Bradford, Riley, Andrews and Isaacs'. After thanking the pianist, they 'wheeled their way through the pleasant country homewards, arriving all safe about 9.30 p.m.'. The report sounds more like an excuse for a rather convivial get-together than a serious cycle ride. One wonders how sober the riders were on the return trip, given it was thought necessary to comment that they arrived 'all safe'! (*Hampshire Advertiser*, 25 July 1891)

July 19th

1766: On this day, the opening of the new theatre in Southampton was celebrated in the *St James's Chronicle or the British Evening Post*:

> We are extremely obliged to the Correspondent who has favoured us with the following copy of the Prologue, spoken by Mr Johnson at the opening of the New Theatre at Southampton.

> ... And can at will call up, as best may suit us / A Cato, Falstaff, Mahomet or Brutus.
> There is locked up my lightning, there my thunder, [points to the roof] / My devils here [points to the floor], for those we must keep under.
> Behind are children ready to be strang'd, / Couples just sit in Love to be entangled,
> Traitors that never on the rack think of pain; / Virgins, oft ravished, that quite chaste remain;
> Women who though they're murdered, still survive; / Nay what's more strange, by often dying, thrive;
> Ghosts that can eat and drink in Poison's spite; / And men who can bear a stabbing ev'ry Night – etc

The flavour of the poem can be appreciated, together with the usual eighteenth-century ironical turn of phrase, in this short extract (the poem actually went on for fifty lines). (*St James's Chronicle or the British Evening Post*)

July 20th

1554: On this day, King Philip of Spain arrived in Southampton for his marriage to Queen Mary of England, daughter of Henry VIII.

Queen Mary was returning the country to the Catholic faith, and this marriage was intended not only to neutralise the ongoing threat of war between England and Spain, but also to strengthen her religious objectives for the country. Philip had sailed into Southampton water escorted by the combined fleets of Spain and England. On his arrival in the town, he went to Holy Rood Church to hear mass. He remained in the town for three days, before continuing his journey to Winchester, where the two reigning monarchs would be married in the cathedral. Queen Mary was so pleased with her reception when she met Philip that she gave Southampton a new sweet wine grant to help their failing foreign trade. This meant that, in the future, all wines from the Levant region would only be landed at Southampton. Unfortunately, this was disputed when the Turkey Company came into being in 1605. A long period of expensive court cases followed, at the end of which the Corporation put their losses as £1,000 and had gained nothing. (J.S. Davies, *A History of Southampton*, Southampton, 1883, pp.258, 357)

JULY 21ST

1938: On this day, the Mayo Composite Aircraft inaugurated commercial mail flights across the North Atlantic Ocean.

Mail to America was still being taken by ship, which was relatively slow in an age where aircraft were developing alongside radio communication. The difficulty lay in the weight of carrying both a cargo and sufficient fuel. However, Mr R.H. Mayo from Imperial Airways at Southampton developed a novel solution – a floatplane carried on the back of a larger aircraft. Using a big flying boat (the Maia) to provide the power to lift itself and the floatplane (Mercury) to a good height, Mercury could then be released from its cradle to complete the journey. By this means, the smaller plane could carry up to 1,000lb weight of mail and fly 3,500 miles, even against a 60mph headwind. It was during take-off that the greatest amount of fuel was needed; therefore, by using the bigger flying boat to provide the power for take-off, the Mercury had the opportunity to carry a large amount of mail without refuelling. So was this where the American space-shuttle idea originated? Can Southampton claim to be part of that programme? Unlikely. (A. Rance (ed.), *Sea Planes and Flying Boats of the Solent*, Southampton, 1981, p.49)

JULY 22ND

1415: On this day, the four plotters conspiring against King Henry V met at Otterbourne, a few miles outside Southampton.

The conspirators were the Earls of March and Cambridge, Lord Scrope, and Sir Thomas Gray. They intended to replace Henry V with Edmund Mortimer, Earl of March, and they met at various places on the outskirts of Southampton during the build-up of the invasion forces going to France. They held another meeting at Hamble on 25 July, and Scrope, Gray and Cambridge met again at the Itchen Ferry. From Gray's confession, it seems that the plan was to make their move against the King either during the voyage to France or just before departure. They met again in Southampton, in Gray's lodgings in the Greyfriars. After that there was a great deal of activity between Cranbury (Otterbourne) and Hamble. It was around this time that Mortimer revealed the plot to the King, who then set a trap for the other three, inviting them to Portchester Castle to discuss the invasion plans. And the consequence? (*See* August 2nd) (T.B. Pugh, *Henry V and the Southampton Plot of 1415*, Southampton, 1988)

JULY 23RD

1806: On this day John Henry Petty, 2nd Marquis of Lansdowne, wrote to Lord Holland from Southampton, describing 'a little accident'.

Petty was descended from the Royal Society President William Petty. William had designed a double-bottomed boat similar to a catamaran, and it seems that his descendant was experimenting with the design, without any ballast, when it overturned. The incident was seen by the scandalous Lady Betty Craven, from a back window of her house. Lady Betty had outraged society by her many affairs, including an affair with the Margrave of Anspach. Providentially for her, her estranged husband (Baron Craven) and the Margravine died about the same time. It was reported that Lady Betty heard of Lord Craven's death on Friday, wore widow's weeds on Saturday, and wore virginal white on Sunday for her marriage to the Margrave. Always the self-publicist, Lady Betty recounts the boat accident in her autobiography, stressing her own role in the rescue. This amounted to her sending her servants out in boats to rescue the Marquis, whilst she waited on the shore with wine 'to refresh the drenched experimentalists ... happy in being instrumental to their preservation'. (*The Beautiful Lady Betty Craven, Vol. II*, 1826, p.142; John Henry Petty correspondence held in British Library; J. Watts, unpublished biography of John Henry Petty, 2nd Marquis of Lansdowne)

July 24th

1646: On this day William Stanley, the Mayor, gave a poor woman 5s towards the ransom needed to release her husband from slavery in Turkey. The Mayor had already paid money towards the release of Walter Long a few months earlier.

Southampton, like many other south coast towns, had suffered at the hands of the Barbary pirates, who attacked shipping not for the cargo but for the people on board. These were taken to become slaves in Algiers and Turkey. The practice continued for over 200 years, and many escaped white slaves passed through Itchenferry village, having returned via the smuggling routes. During 1647, Edmond Cason, the Parliament agent in Algiers, had redeemed four or five men from Southampton. He was forced to pay almost double the original prices he had been told to gain the men's release. These were slaves who were valuable to their owners and probably had useful trades. Ironically, after returning to England some slaves decided that their lives were better in Algiers and went back. (M. South, 'The Southampton Inoculation Campaigns of the Eighteenth Century', unpublished PhD thesis, University of Winchester, 2010, p.126)

JULY 25TH

1884: On this day Richard Parker, from Southampton, was killed at sea. Seventeen-year-old Parker set sail for Australia from Southampton in the yacht *Mignonette*, with Thomas Dudley and two local men, Edmund (Ned) Brooks and Edwin Stephens.

The yacht was wrecked in a storm north of Tristan da Cunha. The four took to the lifeboat, with two tins of turnips and no water. After nineteen days, Parker had lapsed into a coma after drinking seawater; the decision was taken to kill the boy and eat his flesh. The deed was carried out by Dudley and Stephens, and the three men cannibalised Parker's body until rescued by the *Montezuma*. On their return to England, Brooks was allowed to return home, but Dudley and Stephens were tried for murder. It became a landmark case, still quoted today. The judge ruled that 'necessity was no defence for murder', thus outlawing a practice which was regarded as a 'custom of the sea'. After some legal controversies, the two men were given six months' imprisonment. Parker's remains were interred at Jesus Chapel, at Pear Tree Green. Curiously, many years before, Edgar Allan Poe had written a story about four shipwrecked men who drew lots to discover who should be eaten by the others. The fictional victim's name was Richard Parker. (N. Hanson, *The Custom of the Sea: The Story That Changed British Law*, Doubleday, 1999; Edgar Allan Poe, *The Narrative of Arthur Gordon Pym of Nantucket*, 1838)

JULY 26TH

1933: On this day King George V opened the King George V Dry Dock in Southampton.

This was part of the docks extension scheme and was the seventh dry dock to be built there. None of the other six, however, were big enough to accommodate the largest liners of the time. It took two years of building – and the removal of two million tons of earth – before it was completed. Southampton then possessed the largest dry dock in the world, capable of holding liners up to 1,000ft long; it comfortably held the Cunard liner *Queen Mary*. It was, therefore, doubly suitable that King George and Queen Mary both took part in the naming ceremony. They arrived in the royal yacht, the *Victoria and Albert*, which sailed into the new dry dock and was completely dwarfed by its enormous walls. As part of the naming ceremony, Queen Mary poured a glass of wine into the dock! During the era of the big liners, the King George V Dry Dock was the only place where many of the ships could be properly overhauled, and it helped to guarantee work for the docks for many years. (Port Cities Southampton website)

JULY 27TH

1556: On this day, the town received notice that they were to be sent three pirates for hanging.

The Admiralty had captured several pirates, and wished to exploit the situation as much as possible by sending them to different parts of the country for hanging. Instructions were specific: the Admiralty gallows on the seashore should be used, and Captain Jones's body should be left hanging in chains as a warning. The cost of making the chain to hang Jones was 3*s*. (A. Merson, *The Third Book of Remembrance of Southampton, 1514-1602, Vol. II*, Southampton, 1955, pp.56-7)

1785: On this day, the last public hanging at the gallows on the Common took place.

The victim was William Shayer, convicted for having stolen silverware from the home of his previous employer, Mrs Bagenal. Despite pleas for clemency, it was Shayer's bad luck to have been convicted during a national crackdown on crime and the strict application of the law. His body was taken by his family and interred at Bishops Waltham. (J.S. Davies, *A History of Southampton*, Southampton, 1883, p.50)

JULY 28TH

1900: On this day, Netley Hospital was visited as part of an inquiry into conditions in South African military hospitals.

The aim was to question patients who had returned after treatment in South Africa, to establish the quality of care the wounded men had received. Seventy men were questioned, including some recently returned from the Siege of Ladysmith. These men had returned in the *Dunnottar Castle*, landing at Southampton only a few days earlier. On board with them was the young Winston Churchill, who was returning as something of a national hero. He had been sent to report on the Boer War for the *Morning Post*. During his travels, the train he was on had derailed and he was taken prisoner and held in Pretoria for a month. Then he escaped and travelled 300 miles through hostile territory, across Mozambique to Delagoa Bay. He volunteered to join up with British forces which were setting out to relieve the besieged Ladysmith garrison. Churchill was reputed to be one of the first to enter the beleaguered garrison. Despite his audacity and bravery on several occasions, he never received any medal or commendation, as he was officially classified as a civilian. (*Southern Daily Echo*, 28 July 1900)

July 29th

2010: On this day, Caroline Sellex celebrated her hundredth birthday.

Born Caroline Williams, she and her twin sister Matilda were both educated at home in Hamble by the great niece of Horatio Nelson. Both twins were sportswomen, but Caroline was the more successful of the two, being a talented tennis player and also becoming a champion horse rider, winning cups for dressage. The two sisters were motorcycle speedway riders and competed at Southampton in the late 1920s. In 1930, they were racing at Portsmouth when Caroline set a new lap record by slashing twenty-six seconds off the previous best time. It is quite likely that she could have gone on to challenge even the legendary Fay Taylour – who had already done much to get women's dirt-track racing taken seriously by beating most of the UK and international male stars – but in the same year, just as Caroline was reaching her zenith, women were banned from motorcycle racing. (*Southern Daily Echo*, 29 July 2010)

July 30th

1593: On this day, the carrier service between Southampton and London was suspended due to the outbreak of plague in the capital.

The epidemic in London was particularly virulent on this occasion and the town authorities wished to prevent it reaching Southampton by all possible means. All trade with the capital was halted and no goods from the city were to be brought into the town – including baggage – for fear that such items carried the disease. Travelling players coming from areas near London were paid not to come into Southampton, and soldiers marching down from the North in September of the previous year – when the sickness first broke out – avoided London before coming to Southampton to embark. (T. James, *The Third Book of Remembrance of Southampton, 1514-1602, Vol. IV*, Southampton, 1979, pp.14, 74)

JULY 31ST

1831: On this day, Samuel Coldman died in a sewer in St Michael's parish.

Poor Sam was one of the workmen employed to renew the sewer system of the town. This was an attempt to improve the privies in the area. Not very successfully, as it happened, because conditions were still appalling twenty years later; small airless courts, with several families sharing one privy, were still common in large parts of St Michael's parish. Nonetheless, some efforts were being made in 1831 and Sam was working to link up a new sewer with a privy in Butchers Row. When he dug through into the privy recess from the sewer, the stench was so strong that he was overcome and suffocated in the gases that were given off. The smell would have been caused by hydrogen sulphide, a common gas produced by the breakdown of sewage. The gas smells of rotten eggs, is very poisonous and can kill within a short length of time, especially in a confined space. (St Michael's parish burial registers)

AUGUST 1ST

2001: On this day the Saints played their first match in their new stadium.

The new stadium had been a long time in the planning; the original intention had been for it to be located on the outskirts of Southampton, but site restrictions and road access had stopped this plan. The City Council then offered the disused gas works site, a short distance from the club's existing ground at the Dell. It was the ideal solution. The move would take the Saints back to their roots in the centre of the city and put them back in their 'home' parish of St Mary's. There was space for a stadium with just under 33,000 seats – more than twice the capacity of the Dell. The requirements of a modern stadium, and the necessary improvements to the surrounding infrastructure, took the total cost to £32 million. The names of the four main stands in the stadium reflect the surrounding areas of the city – Itchen, Northam, Kingsland and Chapel. To underline the club's links and concerns with the local community, part of the complex provides outside-the-classroom help for youngsters in the area and also houses the Head Office of the Hampshire & Isle of Wight Air Ambulance. (Saints Football Club website; Wikipedia)

August 2nd

1415: On this day the trial of Richard, Earl of Cambridge, Sir Thomas Gray of Northumberland, and Henry, Lord Scrope of Masham, took place at Southampton Castle, where they were imprisoned. They had been plotting to overthrow Henry V and possibly murder him and his brothers.

Gray was tried and executed immediately, but Cambridge and Scrope had demanded to be tried by their peers. Twenty of them were gathered, and the verdict of guilty was passed and carried out immediately. Cambridge, because he was the King's cousin, was spared the indignity of a public execution and was beheaded, without prior hanging. Afterwards, his body and head were interred in St Julian's Church in Winkle Street. Lord Scrope was a Knight of the Garter and had betrayed his trust to his sovereign, so was dealt with more harshly. Henry gave orders that Scrope should be dragged on a hurdle from the castle Watergate, through the town, and outside the Bargate to the place of execution, where he suffered a traitor's death. His head was sent to York and impaled at Micklegate; Gray's had already gone to Newcastle-upon-Tyne. (T.B. Pugh, *Henry V and the Southampton Plot of 1415*, Southampton, 1988)

AUGUST 3RD

1771: On this day, the Corporation heard a case of deodands.

This was the right that the local authorities had to put inanimate or non-human objects on trial, for crimes against a man. On this occasion, the front wheel of William Rogers's stagecoach and the offside horse pulling the coach were being tried. The accused had been responsible for running down and killing Thomas White underneath the Bargate. It's very likely that the coach had been racing one of the other stagecoaches from a rival company. Speed was necessary to maintain the schedule and the reputation of the company. Every company advertised its own coaches' safety, comfort and speed, while slandering the competition. Racing was commonplace, in the town as well as on the open road – in 1775 the Salisbury coach raced into one of the Southampton inns, apparently cornered too fast into the entrance, and capsized. As for the wheel and horse, they were found guilty of the crime and a fine of ten guineas was paid to the Corporation. If Thomas White left a widow, she got nothing – the Corporation was the injured party! (A. Rance, *Southampton: An Illustrated History*, Southampton, 1980; Assembly Book SC2/1/11)

AUGUST 4TH

1900: On this day, Thomas Worsfold was tried for bigamy.

His first marriage had taken place at Wells (Somerset) on 1 August 1897, to a Miss Lansdowne. He then moved to Southampton to 'work', taking lodgings at Firgrove Road and only returning home at the weekends. On 12 July 1900, Worsfold married his landlord's daughter, Elizabeth Terry, and went to 'work' elsewhere on weekends. Worsfold then fled to Birmingham and wrote to both 'wives' from there, whereupon his first wife came to Southampton, visited 'wife' number two, and introduced herself as Worsfold's wife – which was a great shock to poor Miss Terry. But this was probably not as much of a shock as the letter that Worsfold's first (legal) wife received from him, in which he said: 'Do the best you can for yourself and the children and some day I will make it up to you. By the time you get this letter I shall be well on my way to America. Do not grieve for me, but make the best of it. Your broken-hearted husband.' (*Southern Daily Echo*, 4 August 1900)

AUGUST 5TH

1620: On this day, the Pilgrim Fathers set sail from Southampton to seek refuge from religious persecution.

This small group of Independents had previously been forced, under Elizabeth, to leave England and live in Holland, which was more sympathetic to their religion. Now they had briefly returned prior to setting off for the New World, where they could practise their religion without fear of reprisals. They left Southampton in two small vessels, the *Mayflower* and the *Speedwell*. Unfortunately, the *Speedwell* proved less than seaworthy and was obliged to turn back when they reached Plymouth. After transferring all the passengers onto the *Mayflower*, they finally left Plymouth on 6 September, with about 100 souls on board. Other emigrants for the colonies sailed from the port 'for the Barbathoes' and elsewhere. The memorial to the *Mayflower* and the Pilgrim Fathers can be seen at the bottom of the old medieval town. (J.S. Davies, *A History of Southampton*, Southampton, 1883)

AUGUST 6TH

1796: On this day, a cricket match between a Southampton eleven and a Portsmouth eleven was played at Portsmouth; the winners would receive 100 guineas. The match was won by Portsmouth. Sadly, during the game Mr Coulson, playing for Southampton, 'had his eye struck out entirely' by the ball. (*Hampshire Chronicle*, 6 August 1796)

1796: On this day nearly 1,000 French priests, refugees from the French Revolution, arrived from Jersey. They came in eight transport ships and moored in the river. The authorities were immediately sent into consternation and dispatched an express messenger to the Duke of Portland's office for instructions. In the meantime, some of the priests were allowed to come ashore in order to buy provisions. (*Hampshire Chronicle*, 6 August 1796)

AUGUST 7TH

1903: On this day, Buffalo Bill's Wild West show came to town.

It had arrived a few days earlier, using four special trains to accommodate its 800 personnel and 500 horses. Their tour was limited to railway centres and large cities, due to the complexity of moving such large numbers of people, animals and equipment. The whole company set up camp and their display ring on the West Marlands ground (now Watts Park). Here they re-enacted battles from American history and promised realistic military spectacle to the locals. Bucking broncos, Indian war dances and medicine men were all included. Displays of horsemanship were given by an incredible selection of international veteran cavalry groups, including: the Royal English Lancers, Bedouin Arabs, South American Gauchos, United States Cavalry, the Cuban Patriots, Russian Cossacks, Roosevelt Rough Riders, the American Artillery, and Mexican Ruralies. The publicity material trumpeted that this was 'a gathering of extraordinary consequence to fittingly depict all that virile, muscular, heroic manhood has and can endure'. There's nothing new about hype! (*Southern Daily Echo*, 7 August 1903)

AUGUST 8TH

1580: On this day, the Mayor and other officers were assaulted and prevented from holding the Admiralty Court. Traditionally, the court was held at Keyhaven at the high-water mark. The Southampton Mayor (Bernard Cortmill), two aldermen (William Staveley and John Marche) and the Southampton bailiff (Peter Janverin) gathered there, where they met Henry Carew, who was accompanied by three men armed with swords. They:

> ... resisted the foresaid mayor to keep her Majesty's court with violence, reviling the mayor and his officers calling him knave, Jack Squib, rascal and would have thrown the court books into the sea ... and when the officer called the court mocked him with a loud voice ... and stopped the clerk's mouth with his hand ... to the end that he should not proceed [their] quarrelling have broken her Majesty's peace by reason whereof they could not proceed further.

The writer's indignation can still be felt over 400 years later. (R. Anderson, *Letters of the Fifteenth and Sixteenth Centuries*, Southampton, 1922, pp.95-6)

AUGUST 9TH

1787: On this day, at 4 a.m., John Wesley set out in a chaise for Southampton.

He had come to preach to his followers, and on this occasion – which would be his last known visit – he spoke at a school owned by a Mr Fay. Afterwards, Wesley wrote in his journal: 'I believe some of them will not be forgetful hearers, but will bring forth fruit with patience.' Wesley had come to Southampton a number of times, probably combining these trips with visits to his nonconformist friends, the Taylors, at Portswood. On one occasion, when the weather was bad, he requested leave to preach in the Town Hall (Audit House?). The Mayor agreed, and then an hour later took back his promise. Wesley remarked, 'Poor Mayor!' There is a possibly apocryphal story that in 1790, aged eighty-seven, Wesley was crossing to Southampton on the Isle of Wight ferry when the boat was upset and the passengers were left in the water for an hour, until a passing boat going to Ryde picked them up. He was said to have borne the ordeal with fortitude and resignation. (*Southern Daily Echo*, 13 May 2008)

August 10th

1889: On this day, Princess Beatrice came to lay the foundation stone for the new headquarters of the Gordon Boys' Brigade in Ogle Road. Flags and flowers decorated the route from the Royal Pier, where the princess and her husband had arrived in the royal yacht; all the ships were dressed and the whole town joined in the celebrations.

The town branch of the Gordon Boys' Brigade had been established as a memorial to General Charles Gordon, Governor General of the Sudan during the 1884 uprising, where he had been killed. Gordon lived with his parents and sister at the family home, 5 Rockstone Place. When he was there, it was not unusual to see him smoking his pipe outside the house; in winter he retired to the cellar with it. He was forbidden to smoke indoors. Gordon's adherence to truth made his life difficult when he wished to avoid company. He had been known to excuse himself by saying that he had to go to London, but, rather than tell a lie, he would then take a pointless journey to London. After his death the family did not want statues erected, but preferred something that would reflect his philanthropic ideals, and so the idea of the Gordon Boys was born. (*See* January 14th) (*Daily Echo* archive, 10 August 1889; M. Taylor, 'Gordon of Khartoum', *Southampton: Gateway to the British Empire*, London, 2007)

AUGUST 11TH

1827: On this day, the Southampton Regatta from the previous Monday and Tuesday was reported upon.

The accustomed mixture of expensive yachts and fishing boats from the village of Itchenferry took part in their different classes. Six fishing boats took part, sailing from Southampton Town Quay to Netley Abbey and back again. Unsurprisingly, Jasper Diaper, from one of the acclaimed Itchenferry sailing families, won the race. Later there was a ladies' rowing race, when the report read thus:

> Almost the best part of the Regatta was the boat race for the women – four pullers and a hen-swain we suppose we must call the steers-woman. We cannot enlarge on this most popular race, more than to say, it was contested by four boats, and won by Ann Diaper and her female friends, who are all, we presume, better known in the fish-market and at Itchenferry than to any of our readers.

I wonder if such a report would be printed in 2012? (*The Morning Post*, 13 August 1827)

AUGUST 12TH

1608: On this day, Judith Brading and Walter Bands' wife were to be whipped.

Judith was a self-confessed prostitute and Walter Bands' wife had been punished for bawdry on an earlier occasion. Bands seems to have maintained her innocence this time, but the case against her was nonetheless considered to have been proved. It is possibly the difference in their attitudes towards their crimes which produced two different methods of administering the punishment. Mistress Bands was to be whipped at the cart's tail through the town. Judith Brading, on the other hand, would be whipped behind closed doors in the Town Hall. Whipping was a duty of the Town Crier, and the victim was stripped to the waist (modesty was not an issue at this time) for the punishment to be administered. Those sentenced to be punished at the 'cart's tail' had their hands tied to the back of a horse and cart, which was then led on a prescribed route through the town, visiting the most crowded areas, like markets. The Crier was paid fourpence per whipping. Judith was to remain a problem for the town authorities. (J. Horrocks, *Assembly Books of Southampton, Vol. I, 1602-1608*, Southampton, 1917, p.76)

August 13th

1864: On this day, two lions escaped from a visiting menagerie based on West Marlands.

The show had been there for two weeks, but this evening two of the animals made a bid for freedom. One was quickly recaptured, but the lioness slipped through the net, moved across the open ground – it had cleared of people in a very short length of time – and headed towards Havelock Terrace. Finding the gate open and the front door ajar, she took refuge inside. Her pursuers quickly closed the door to keep her locked up until the keepers arrived. Meanwhile, the owner of the house had seen the lioness running along the road and sent his servant to secure the front door. On meeting the lion in the passage, she ran and locked herself in the kitchen. The owner and his family took refuge in an upstairs room, while the keepers brought a 'shifting den' through the downstairs room window and, having stunned the beast with an iron bar, trussed it up and got it into the carrying cage, finally taking the lioness back to the menagerie in triumph. (*Hampshire Independent*, 17 August 1864)

AUGUST 14TH

1552: On this day the young King Edward VI came to the town. He arrived with a retinue of 150 people, who had to be accommodated. While here, he left the only existing account of the town as seen through royal eyes: 'The citizens had bestowed for our coming great cost in painting, repairing and rampairing their walls. The town is handsome and for the bigness of it has as fair houses as be in London. The citizens made great cheer and many of them keep costly tables.' (J.S. Davies, *A History of Southampton*, Southampton, 1883, p.480)

———•◆•———

1967: On this day, 100-year-old Mrs Addie recalled monumental events she had witnessed in her life, such as seeing Queen Victoria and the effect of the *Titanic* disaster on the town.

Mrs Addie had been a widow for fifty years and, since the depression in the 1920s, had supported herself by making dust caps for housewives. When permed hair became fashionable women did not want to wear the caps, but she contracted to make caps for the workforce of Hartley's Jams. Working at home, on her treadle sewing machine, she produced 6,000 caps every year for many years. (*Southern Daily Echo*)

AUGUST 15TH

1642: On this day the town was in a state of alert, as the Parliamentarian army were in the area. Special watches were set up around the town. Twenty-four men were to muster at the market house at 7 p.m. at the sound of the drum, and to remain on duty until 6 a.m. Six were to be at the Eastgate, with four more in East Street, and another six were to be Above Bar. During the hours of daylight, eight different men were to muster at the Assembly at the sound of the drum. The town's attitude towards the warring factions of the Civil War are best described as lukewarm. Fewer than half of the Assembly were sympathetic towards the Parliamentarians, making the authorities nominally Royalist. Their 'special watch' security seems rather lukewarm as well. (Assembly Books, SC 2/1/6, 15 August 1642)

1803: On this day a cricket match was held on Pear Tree Green, between Southampton Cricket Club and Itchenferry village. Southampton was beaten in one innings, by a number of runs. A large number of people attended, and booths serving 'cold collations and every kind of liquor for the entertainment of the parties and their guests' were available. Southampton's cricket team was consistent – it lost! (*Hampshire Chronicle*, 22 August 1803)

AUGUST 16TH

1940: On this day, Flight Lieutenant James Nicolson was shot at and 'captured' by the Home Guard at Millbrook.

Nicolson had been in combat, over Southampton, in his Hurricane fighter. After dismissing an opposing fighter, his own aircraft was hit by four cannon shells, wounding him and setting fire to the gravity tank. With flames in the cockpit, he was just about to bale out when he sighted another enemy aircraft. This he attacked and shot down, despite suffering burns to his hands, face and legs. After eventually baling out, he landed at Millbrook, where an over-excited member of 'Dad's Army' took a shot at him. As a result of his action, Nicolson was awarded Fighter Command's only Victoria Cross of the Second World War. (Victoria Cross holders online; A. Rance, *Southampton: An Illustrated History*, Southampton, 1980, p.164)

AUGUST 17TH

1519: On this day, the town's curates complained to the Mayor about the quality of the candles being made for the churches by the town chandlers.

In an effort to cut costs, they had been using adulterated wax and second-rate wicks, with the following results: 'by means of making false wax … in mixing resin and turpentine with the same in tapers and candles, not only the images, vestments and altar cloths be greatly hurted but also … very noxious to all parishioners being in the churches at their divine services.' The Mayor took this very seriously, and the chandlers were ordered to use only clean, white wax with white wicks, not black ones. Moreover, they were to put their marks on the candles so that anyone making poor-quality candles could be traced. For any first offence, the fraudster would spend six days and six nights in gaol; for the second offence, they would spend three market days sat in the stocks; while a third offence meant banishment from the town. The Mayor, and various members of the Corporation as witnesses, signed the agreement, and the marks of five barbers were added. Presumably the chandlers were also the town barbers. (A. Merson, *The Third Book of Remembrance of Southampton, 1514-1602, Vol. I,* Southampton, 1952)

AUGUST 18TH

1934: On this day, the greyhounds at the Banister Court Stadium caught the mechanical hare!

During the hurdles event, with the four runners halfway round the course, the hare unaccountably slowed down slightly. The two leading greyhounds immediately pounced on it and quickly had it off the carriage. The other two dogs continued running, which gave rise to the question: Do the greyhounds really run with the hare as their objective, or simply dash round the course by instinct? There may be another reason – the trailing greyhounds saw this as an opportunity to win the race, while their rivals were busy with the hare! (*Southern Daily Echo*)

AUGUST 19TH

1899: On this day, it was reported that Prince Lobengula, from Matabeleland, and his bride were in Southampton.

They were staying at a hotel near to the Royal Pier, possibly for about three weeks, before sailing for Durban. This was considered newsworthy as the twenty-four-year-old prince had married twenty-one-year-old Miss Katie Jewell, who was English. They had been obliged to marry at a registry office, as the Church had declared the marriage to be 'an act of stupendous stupidity and immorality' and refused to sanction it. The prince responded by saying that he considered he had been very badly treated, because in his country plenty of Englishmen married native women; moreover, the couple had had to suffer accusations of bigamy made against him. In the eighteenth century, when a local black man married a local white girl such attitudes were never considered. The wedding was carried out at South Stoneham Church and their first child was baptised at the nonconformist chapel in Portswood. (*Huddersfield Chronicle and West Yorkshire Advertiser*; *Jackson's Oxford Journal*; South Stoneham parish registers)

August 20th

1945: On this day, the *Queen Elizabeth* made her first visit to Southampton, more than six years after her completion on Clydebank.

Since then, she had been serving as a troopship, and she continued in service until the following March. During this time, she returned Canadian troops to Canada and brought back German prisoners of war. One other item that returned to Southampton on board the *Queen Elizabeth* was the Magna Carta. When things were looking a bit bleak during the Second World War, the document had been shipped to Fort Knox for safekeeping; now it was quietly returned to England. Her service to the national cause completed, the '*Lizzie*' was completely refitted in Southampton's Graving Dock and, at last, on 26 October 1946, she sailed on her maiden voyage to America with more than 2,000 passengers on board. Her sister ship, *Queen Mary*, resumed her passenger liner role in July 1947, following her final wartime mission ferrying 9,000 GI brides and their children to New York from the UK. The return of the Queens signalled the return of Southampton's role as a passenger port and 'Gateway to England'. (A. Rance, *Southampton: An Illustrated History*, Southampton, 1980, p.177)

AUGUST 21ST

1982: On this day, the Cutty Sark Tall Ships' Race finished at Southampton.

There were three separate legs on this occasion; American ships raced one another from Venezuela to Lisbon, the Europeans sailed against one another from Falmouth to Lisbon, and then the combined group raced from Lisbon to Southampton. The first Tall Ships' Race had taken place in 1956 from Torbay to Lisbon, but its origins go back even further – to the tea clippers racing for home from China. It had been an unofficial competition to bring the season's first crop of tea back to London, but in 1866 extra incentives were added, when there was heavy betting on the ships. The winning vessel was awarded an extra £1 for every ton of tea delivered, and the captain of the winning clipper was given a percentage of the ship's earnings. Nowadays, the race is intended to promote the 'education and development of young people of all nationalities, religions and social backgrounds through sail training', and to that end the most coveted award is the Cutty Sark Trophy. This has nothing to do with winning, but is awarded to the vessel which, in the opinion of the masters, has done the most to promote international friendship and understanding during the event. (Official 1982 Cutty Sark Tall Ships' Race programme)

AUGUST 22ND

1935: On this day Warrior died, aged twenty-six.

The big white gelding, over sixteen hands high, had served as a police horse since 1919. Named Warrior because of its service throughout the First World War, the horse was renowned for its gentleness and was a popular sight in the town, especially with the children. During the horse's war service, which began when it was shipped to France in 1914, Warrior had served with the Old Contemptibles and been involved in several notable actions. These included the retreat from Mons and the advance upon Aisne, where the horse was wounded in the shoulder by shrapnel and carried the scar for the rest of its life. On recovery, Warrior returned to duty and survived until the Armistice; then, with all other surviving horses, it was returned to England to be sold off. Miss Hilda Moore bought the gelding and presented it to the town, where it became a police horse. On Warrior's death, Sir Sidney Kimber (a prominent member of the council) was horrified to hear that the body was destined for the knacker's yard. Instead, he arranged for Warrior to be buried on the newly opened golf course. The headstone and garden are on the path adjacent to the eighteenth hole. (Ian Broad, *The Illustrated Guide to Southampton*, 1982; Warrior's gravestone inscription)

AUGUST 23RD

1897: On this day, the arrangements for a chess tournament were announced.

It was expected to be a first-class competition, with several top-class London amateurs taking part. The tournament was part of the summer meeting of the Southern Counties Chess Association; entries needed to be in before 27 August as the meeting would be held on 30 August. There would be several minor tournaments and handicaps, but there would also be an innovative competition – a special tournament for ladies! (*Daily News*)

AUGUST 24TH

1988: On this day, the suburb of Swaythling advertised the largest street party in the world.

Plans were being made to hold the event on Saturday 27 August, prior to the opening of the new Portswood bypass, Thomas Lewis Way. The road would allow traffic to bypass Swaythling and its neighbouring suburb of Portswood when travelling from the M27 to Southampton's city centre. The organisers estimated that, before it was officially opened, the new road could hold a street party for about 10,000 people. This would break the previous *Guinness World Records* figure for the world's largest street party by a generous margin. Entertainers and local bands were preparing for the event, and tables and chairs were organised – although more would probably be needed. Visitors were encouraged to bring their own, if possible. Last, but not least, they had arranged for a helicopter to fly over and record the event, between 10 a.m. and 1 p.m. Saturday came and so did the rain. The organisers said that everything that could go wrong did go wrong. Only 3,000 brave souls came, and the record for London's Oxford Street (5,500 people) still stands. (*Southern Daily Echo*, 24 August 1988)

AUGUST 25TH

1844: On this day, a large consignment of guano from Ichaboe Island was unloaded at Southampton Docks. It had been imported by John Boyd & Co. in London, and two agents in the High Street were employed to sell the guano locally.

Ichaboe, lying just off the west coast of Africa, had been discovered in 1828 by Captain B. Morrell, who reported 'birds' manure to the depth of twenty-five feet'. Its use as a fertiliser was unparalleled and the 'guano rush' began. At its height, in 1844-1845, there were no less than 450 boats lying off the small island, while 6,000 men were scraping guano. Guano had built up over centuries from the droppings of the island's seabird population. The word is derived from the Spanish for 'dung'. This shipment, carried by the ship *Blucher*, filled several dock warehouses and was declared to have 'an unusual extent of fertilising matter and had been analysed by an experimental chemist of the highest competency'. This amazing product would be sold at £9 per ton, or a hundredweight sample bag costing 12s. There was no charge for the bags. (Avian demography unit, Ichaboe Island Namibia website; *Hampshire Independent*, 24 August 1844; 31 August 1844)

August 26th

1796: On this day, the Chevalier D'Eon was seriously wounded during an exhibition fencing match at Southampton.

The Chevalier D'Eon was notorious because he dressed as a woman and there was considerable speculation about his sex. In London, he was partnered in his fencing demonstrations with Mrs Bateman, an actress and female fencer. It appears, however, that in Southampton on this occasion he was partnered by a French male compatriot. The wound was not fatal, but cut the armpit tendons and prevented him from fencing again.

Born into the French nobility (1728-1810), Charles Geneviève Auguste André Timothée D'Eon de Beaumont became a career soldier and diplomatist, and was awarded the royal and military order of St Louis for his services as a spy. It was during his exploits as a spy that he adopted women's clothing. Later on, when he fell from favour with the French authorities, he was forbidden to wear his military uniform and compelled to appear as a woman at all times. After the accident at Southampton, he retired to live in obscurity in London with a Mrs Cole, who believed him to be a woman and collapsed with shock after the post-mortem proclaimed that his male organs were 'perfectly formed'. (Dictionary of National Biography online)

August 27th

1669: On this day, the Corporation made plans for King Charles II's visit to the town on his royal progress.

As usual, the Corporation was concerned about the expenses involved, and agreed to present the King with a purse containing just £50, estimating that the total costs would be £100, including the gift. The purse was accepted when the King entered the Bargate the following Monday evening. The castle had been demolished many years earlier, therefore the royal party was accommodated in the homes of Corporation members; the King stayed with Mr Richbell in the High Street. Remaining in the town for the next week, the party enjoyed themselves in the surrounding area with hunting expeditions in the New Forest (where the King killed a stag) and boat trips on the River Itchen, using both private boats and the public Itchen ferries. It was in Southampton that the King received news of the death of the Queen Mother; he made an unexpectedly early departure, rising before daybreak to take a coach by 4 a.m. The town had intended a farewell banquet, 'but through his Majesty's sudden departure this was omitted'. Is there a sigh of relief detected in the recorded comment? (J.S. Davies, *A History of Southampton*, Southampton, 1883)

AUGUST 28TH

1682: On this night the bells of All Saints' Church were stolen.

The old medieval church of All Saints had a peal of five bells, but sometime between midnight on 28 August and early morning on 29 August, three of the church bells were stolen from the tower. How it was possible to unhook and lower three great bells quietly and without mishap in the dark is surprising enough, but then they were apparently transported out through the Bargate as well. Despite the hue and cry that went up, a report in the *London Gazette* the following month, and the offer of a reward for information given to the Mayor by 'persons having any knowledge of the whereabouts of the bells or of those who committed the theft', no information was forthcoming. The bells had disappeared into thin air. In 1715 the parish admitted that the bells were not going to be found and the Corporation gave them £10 towards the cost of the new ones. However, it may be worth noting that recently some slight evidence for a bell foundry, approximately in the area of the West Quay shopping centre, has been found. What better place to hide them? (E. Sandell, 'Song of the Bells', *Southampton Sketches*, Southampton, 1977; All Saints' parish registers)

August 29th

1908: On this day, Southampton hosted part of the Olympics.

Rome should have hosted the Olympics, but Vesuvius had erupted and decimated Naples in 1906, which meant that much of the town had to be rebuilt and Italy felt unable to afford the Olympics as well. London stepped into the breach and built White City Stadium to stage most events. It was, however, the first Games to stage events at other venues – and Southampton was chosen as a suitable site for a new event: motorboat racing. A course was marked out, in Southampton Water, for the three 40-mile races. The event was to take place during 28 and 29 August, with just six entrants – five British and one French – who were all expected to achieve speeds of about 19mph. Unfortunately, there was a gale blowing on the 28th and only one race was completed, won by the Frenchman. On the second day conditions improved slightly, and 'Tom' Thornycroft won both remaining races in his boat *Girinus*. Neither race was hotly contested because no other contestants finished the course. Ultimately, the Olympic Committee considered the use of mechanical machines not to be in the Olympic spirit and motorboat racing was dropped. (*Daily Echo*, 7 August 2008)

AUGUST 30TH

1438: On this day the town steward, John Cawse, paid the costs for the lion which had been in the town's care for nine weeks.

Costs included not only its food, but also making a collar, chain and staples, together with a special cart for its transportation to London. Two horses were needed for the cart, and the lion's keeper, Louis Morew, needed someone to accompany him on the journey. Other expenses had to be paid to the boatman taking the lion and Louis across the river. The care taken to ensure the lion's safe arrival in London indicates that it was one of the North African lions (a species now extinct) destined for the royal menagerie in the Tower of London. Henry I had started the first royal zoo at Woodstock; during Henry III's reign the collection was moved to the Tower, where it stayed until 1828, when it was transferred to Regents Park (forming the basis of the present Zoological Gardens). In Southampton, it seems likely that the lion was kept near to the inn which was later called the Lion Inn. (H. Gidden, *Steward's Books of Southampton 1434-39, Vol. II*, Southampton, 1939)

AUGUST 31ST

1936: On this day, the *Queen Mary* won the Blue Riband for the fastest crossing in both directions between New York and Cherbourg. The voyage began and ended at Southampton, but, due to speed restrictions in the Solent, this could not be the official start and finish point.

The Blue Riband was the prize awarded to the ship which made the fastest crossing of the North Atlantic. To gain the trophy, a liner had to beat both eastward and westward record times, on the same voyage. The actual award was the Hales Trophy, and the Blue Riband pennant itself was flown by the holder. Intense rivalry between the *Mary* and the French *Normandie* liner developed, with the ships regularly breaking one another's record and exchanging congratulatory telegrams, ending 'until next time'. In August 1938, the *Mary* regained the trophy and held it until 1952. During the war years, her speed was put to use as a troopship. Painted grey, she travelled unescorted as no other ship could match her speed; she became known as the 'Grey Ghost'. (C. Bailey, *Down the Burma Road*, Southampton, 1990; Blue Riband website)

SEPTEMBER 1ST

1609: On this day, Mr James Courtney at last complained to the Town Assembly about the injustice he felt regarding the lease for his property.

He was the tenant of the house or tower above the Watergate and it was annoying him that the lease was still in the previous owner's name, despite the fact that he, Courtney, had been paying it for many years. He therefore requested that the lease should be altered and put into his own name. The Assembly agreed and, two weeks later, he collected a new lease in his own name – after paying a suitable fee to the town, of course. (J. Horrocks, *Assembly Books of Southampton, Vol. II, 1609-1610*, Southampton, 1920, pp.56, 58)

1866: On this day another injustice over land use was corrected. The ratepayers of Portswood were at last allowed to graze their cattle on the Common in the same way that those ratepayers in the walled town, All Saints' parish, St Mary's parish and Shirley had been allowed to do for many years past. (*Hampshire Telegraph & Sussex Chronicle*)

SEPTEMBER 2ND

1378: On this day, the 'mind' of William Malmesyll and his wife Margaret was established at St Michael's Church.

The 'mind' of William and Margaret meant their care for the community, and a day set aside to remember them both. For this, William had set up a charity which was distributed annually on this date. While setting up charities associated with a church or chantry was not unusual, William's was rather different because payments were made to a broad spectrum of people. These included the five curates of the five parish churches, the five clerks of the churches, the Mayor, the town steward, and the bedman (inmate of an almshouse). Additionally, money was to be distributed directly to the poor, along with three dozen loaves, two dozen ale, three cheeses and a gallon of wine. The expenditure on the anniversary is noted in the town steward's accounts for 1428/9, which seems to indicate that the funds had run out but the annual distribution was maintained by the Corporation. (J.S. Davies, *A History of Southampton*, Southampton, 1883, p.424)

September 3rd

1986: On this day, Baron Maybray-King died in Royal South Hants Hospital, aged eighty-five.

Horace King had been born near Middlesbrough and, after gaining his English degree from Oxford, came to Southampton to teach. He was awarded a PhD from King's College in 1940. His writing was diverse, and included topics from Homer to Sherlock Holmes. King joined the Labour Party in Southampton and was elected to the House of Commons in 1950. He arrived at Parliament the first time wearing a cloth cap in memory of James Keir Hardie, founder of the Independent Labour Party. An active member of the House, he was the first Labour member to become speaker. He established his authority with a headmasterly and avuncular approach. He retired as speaker in 1970 and became a life peer, Baron Maybray-King, attending the House of Lords and becoming deputy speaker there. There were a number of surprising aspects of his character. In Southampton he tended to appear as a very traditional figure, but in Westminster he was well known in the bars, and had even switched on the Blackpool Illuminations. Moreover he was a good pianist, played the piano-accordion, and loved entertaining children. (Dictionary of National Biography online)

SEPTEMBER 4TH

1820: On this day the town's first gasometer was completed. It would dominate the skyline along the River Itchen for many years to come.

After its completion, the town had gas street lighting within a few weeks. The iron pillars to support the gas lights were provided by William Chamberlayne, one of the MPs for the borough. He was also a large shareholder in the Gas Company, so may have had more than a passing interest in its expansion. Whatever his motives, the gift was greatly appreciated by the inhabitants and the Corporation. To reflect their gratitude, in August 1822 a large iron column, surmounted by an urn, was erected at the corner of Northam Bridge Road and Above Bar to commemorate Chamberlayne's generosity. Seven years later the column was moved to Town Quay, as an aid to local navigation. When its role became redundant, it was moved again and for many years was in the centre of a traffic roundabout, near Hoglands Park. More recently it has been moved, yet again, and at present is sited in Houndwell Park. (J.S. Davies, *A History of Southampton*, Southampton, 1883, p.514; A. Rance, *Southampton: An Illustrated History*, Southampton, 1980, p.129)

SEPTEMBER 5TH

1779: On this day, a parson preaching on the Isle of Wight was handed a note which caused him to leap out of his pulpit, run outside and fire the beacon, so throwing the entire Island into panic.

During the American War of Independence, France and Spain had joined forces to support America against Britain. Fears of invasion by the French had reached a peak in 1779. The French plan was to land on the Isle of Wight, simultaneously invading Portsmouth. Then, having successfully neutralised the Royal Navy, they would march on London. Messenger Monsey, a physician writing from Southampton, recorded the parson's reaction and reported the local consternation: 'I fear that the Southampton Governor was as much, if not more, alarmed than the rest of the inhabitants, which is not very clever.' Sightings of the combined fleet were reported all along the south coast, but the invasion never came. The French and Spanish sailors were dying from typhus and smallpox so fast that the ships could not be manned properly, and they limped back home. So many bodies were thrown overboard that locals refused to eat fish for months, for fear of being poisoned. (A. Patterson, *The Other Armada*, Manchester, 1960, pp.37-58; C. Haydon, 'A Letter from Southampton, September 1779', *Proceedings of the Hampshire Field Club and Archaeological Society, Vol. 41*, 1985, pp.284-7)

September 6th

1558: On this day, Lord St John reported to Queen Elizabeth on the sickness in the area.

St John was the Governor of the Isle of Wight and lived at Netley, near Southampton. From here he received news from the Isle of Wight and Portsmouth, as well as Southampton. The picture he painted was a sorry one; more than half the population was sick, fields were unharvested, other crops were neglected and work was almost at a standstill. The Governor had a house guest, Dr John Jones, who also caught the disease. Jones later reported on the course of the sickness, saying he had suffered an extreme fever and sweating for two to three weeks, and was convalescent for three months before being fully recovered. These reports were the result of a long-running influenza pandemic, which continued throughout the country for three years, from 1556-1559. The debilitated labour force meant reduced food supplies, widespread hunger, and weakened recruits for the army and navy. Even when the survivors had recovered, the workforce was considerably reduced and it is possible that the influenza outbreaks had a disastrous effect on the Elizabethan economy for a long period. (C. Creighton, *A History of Epidemics in Britain, Vol. I*, pp.403-4)

SEPTEMBER 7TH

1625: On this day, in Southampton, King Charles I signed
The Treaty of Southampton between England and the United
Provinces of the Netherlands, in which they became allies
against their common enemy, Spain.

Due to the widespread outbreak of plague in London,
Parliament had left the capital and adjourned to Oxford, where
they had stayed for a few days at the beginning of August.
Then King Charles and his council left that city and came to
Southampton. Here they continued to carry on the affairs
of State, with the King apparently staying at No. 17 High
Street. They remained in the town for some considerable
time, at the end of which the King was indebted to the town
Corporation, as well as that of Salisbury, for the £3,000 worth
of expenses incurred by his household. (J.S. Davies, *A History
of Southampton*, Southampton, 1883)

September 8th

1569: On this day Queen Elizabeth was staying at Southampton Castle, where she wrote a writ removing the Mayor of Coventry. A plot against Elizabeth, by Mary Queen of Scots, had been discovered while Mary was held at Coventry. The Mayor had been careless.

Elizabeth had broken her journey from Titchfield to Basing to stay in Southampton and, as usual, was on a fundraising mission. The Mayor, John Crooke, presented her with a purse containing £40. The purse had been purchased in London and cost 30s, but a local woman, Margaret Primer, received another shilling to finish off the bottom before it was given to the Queen. Elizabeth's visits were always expensive; she required entertaining and the town also had to pay members of her household, including her bearward, sergeant-at-arms, footmen, trumpeters, marshal, yeomen of the mail, yeomen of the bottles, and her porters. Then there were the musicians, drums and flute from Portsmouth, a local musician, minstrels and skylors (squealers or bagpipes). The archery butts had to be repaired and new bows made for her use; the gunners were paid for firing a salute; the town mace had to be re-gilded; and the town officials bought new liveries. The total, excluding feasting, came to £70. No wonder the Queen's visits were considered a mixed blessing. (C. Butler, *The Book of Fines: Annual Accounts of the Mayors of Southampton, Vol. II, 1540-1571*, Southampton, 2009, pp.76-8; J.S. Davies, *A History of Southampton*, Southampton, 1883, p.480)

SEPTEMBER 9TH

2011: On this day David Welch was installed as the new Knight-of-the-Green, on the Old Bowling Green in the town. From this time forward, while on the Bowling Club premises, he was to be addressed as Sir David.

Bowls has been played on the site since before 1299, making it the oldest site still in use. The Knighthood Competition is believed to have been inaugurated in August 1776, by a Mr Miller, aged eighty-two. This makes it one of the oldest competitions in the world, which is reflected in its rules. All members of the Bowling Club who have not won the competition previously (Gentlemen Commoners) are eligible to take part, but the Knights themselves are excluded. The competition takes place in August and may continue for several days, being played over the whole of the green, unrestricted by the rink line and boundaries. Organisation and supervision are the responsibility of all previous winners (the Knights), who officiate in their frock coats and top hats. (Southampton Old Bowling Green website)

September 10th

1890: On this day the Mayor and magistrates called for troops from Portsmouth to restore order.

Negotiations between the dockers and the employers had broken down, and a strike had begun for recognition of the Union two days before, with dockers, coal-porters, seamen and ships' firemen in the port stopping work at midnight and posting pickets at the gates. By morning a large crowd had gathered, completely blocking the road and railway lines, stopping all traffic entering or leaving the docks. The crowd became a mob which the police charged repeatedly, without result. The troops came from Portsmouth and cleared a small space after being ordered to 'fix bayonets'. The troops were attacked with stones and bottles. The army officer complained that he wouldn't have his men knocked about, and issued live ammunition. Some officials demanded that they fire on the mob, but the Mayor called in the fire brigade, who cleared the road with fire hoses, allowing troops to occupy it. The mob turned their anger against the Mayor and demolished his shop. More troops arrived and the Admiralty sent two gun-boats to prevent pickets entering via the docks. Eventually feelings cooled down, the Union was recognised, the docks returned to normality and the Mayor opened another shop – in Portsmouth. (A. Patterson, *A History of Southampton 1700-1914, Vol. III*, Southampton, 1975, pp.90-3; *Southampton Times*, 13 September 1890; *Hampshire Advertiser*, 29 November 1890)

September 11th

1858: On this day an excursion train to Salisbury ran, with passengers paying 1s 6d return. The train comprised twenty-five carriages and 'the weather was very favourable for the excursionists'. (*Hampshire Telegraph & Sussex Chronicle*)

———◆———

1858: On this day the inauguration of the Channel Islands telegraph was celebrated, with the first message sent from Jersey to Southampton and then on to London. Naturally the first message was a congratulatory one to His Majesty! A beautiful instrument had been fixed at the Southampton telegraph office for the working of the new line. Expenses for the completion of the line were £25,000, which had been helped by a government grant of 6 per cent for twenty-five years on the grand total of £30,000.

SEPTEMBER 12TH

1809: On this day the owner of the Gothic Castle, John Henry Petty, 2nd Marquis of Lansdowne, presented the town with a statue of George III.

The statue was to be sited in the niche on the south side of the Bargate, above the central arch and beneath the sundial. The existing occupant of the niche, Queen Anne, was ejected and relegated to an alcove inside the Bargate itself. There she languished for over 100 years, until dragged out to take part in riotous celebrations during VE day. The popular story goes that she had to be rescued from a bonfire, and during the process lost one arm.

———◆———

1892: On this day, the wealthy local yachtsman Sidney Watson was cremated. At this time, England's first (and for a while only) crematorium was at Woking, and a special train was hired to take the coffin, relatives and friends there. After the cremation, his ashes remained at Woking for a year whilst his tomb was erected at Southampton. (J.S. Davies, *A History of Southampton*, Southampton, 1883; Friends of Southampton Old Cemetery Newsletter, July 2007)

September 13th

1931: On this day the Schneider Trophy for seaplanes was won outright by Britain, when the Supermarine S6b floatplane achieved a speed of 340.08mph. Six days later, the same aircraft reached 407.5mph, over a measured course, setting a new world record.

Jacques Schneider, a French industrialist and entrepreneur, set up the contest in 1913, when it was won by France with a speed of 45.75mph. If a country won the trophy on three consecutive occasions, it became their property and the competition was finished. Over eighteen years twelve races were held, and initially six countries took part, but after the First World War, when the competition was resumed, Germany dropped out. In 1913, Noel Pemberton-Billing established his Supermarine company in Southampton, on the River Itchen. Thanks to the flair of his designer, R.J. Mitchell, the winning airframe designs came into being. Britain won the 1927 race in Venice; the race at Calshot in 1929 with a four-sided course around the Solent; and won a third time in 1931, using a triangular route in the Solent. R.J. Mitchell went on to design the Spitfire, using many of the lessons he had learnt from the winning S6b Schneider Trophy design. (D. Molden (ed.), *The Schneider Trophy Contest, 1913-1931*, Southampton, 1981)

SEPTEMBER 14TH

1844: On this day the town's drainage system was causing concern again. The Sewer Committee was given instructions to obtain estimates and confer with the owners of the land adjacent to St Mary's glebe lands. This land was surrounded by a stinking ditch that flooded whenever there was any rain and deposited its filth across the fields.

Areas across the town were very insanitary, with no clean water or adequate sewage arrangements. As a result, the sewers were likely to flood and the drains to back up. This state of affairs lasted until the 1880s and 1890s, when Mr James Lemon became the Borough Engineer. It was due to his efforts that the health of the town was considerably improved. He undertook not only the much-needed slum clearance, but more importantly he carried out a radical overhaul and rebuilding of the sewage system. This meant that there was almost no contamination of the fresh water supply, and the occurrence of cholera and typhoid was greatly reduced. Although he was knighted and became Sir James Lemon, few people realise that Lemon Road at Shirley is named after one of the town's greatest benefactors and not a fruit! (*Hampshire Telegraph & Sussex Chronicle*, 14 September 1844; *Hampshire Advertiser*, 2 April 1890)

SEPTEMBER 15TH

1478: On this day, Peter Jacobson and Roland Hoke both complained to the Piepowder Court about being threatened with violence.

The Piepowder Court had its origins in the town fairs and markets, when strangers could be tried by a temporary court set up for the market days, or bring cases against residents of the town if they felt they had been dealt with unfairly. The name derived from the French *pieds poudreux* ('dusty feet') courts, due to the association with people walking to market. In Southampton, however, with almost continual comings and goings of trading ships and merchants, the Piepowder Court sat much more frequently and ultimately became almost as important a part of the town's jurisdiction process as the Common Court. So what violence was threatened that alarmed Jacobson and Hoke so much? Both swore an 'oath on his body that he was put in fear of his life and the mutilation of his members'. It is easy to appreciate how alarming this threat must have been. (T. Olding, *The Common and Piepowder Courts of Southampton, 1426-1483*, Southampton, Part I, 2011, pp.136-7)

September 16th

1594: On this day William Hopgood was examined about a charge of witchcraft brought against Widow Wells. Hopgood's evidence reported an incident which had taken place at his house five years previously.

Widow Wells had come to his door in the morning and again in the afternoon, hoping for some bread. She had sat silently waiting for a long time, but he had given her nothing and she had gone away. This happened the next day as well. On the third day, at about the same time, she did not come, but five or six young, healthy pigs suddenly began to behave strangely, dancing and leaping as if they had been bewitched. This continued for two hours, at the end of which they had all died. Hopgood was convinced that this was caused by Widow Wells, and when she next came for relief he stopped his servants from giving her anything. He then accused her of witchcraft and forbade her from coming to his house again, or he would have her burned as a witch. She denied his accusations, but kept away from his house afterwards. A sad tale reflecting how coincidence (the pigs had probably eaten something poisonous), fear and superstition could affect a community. (E. Aubrey and G. Hamilton, *Books of Examinations and Depositions 1570-1594*, Southampton, 1914, p.158)

SEPTEMBER 17TH

1620: On this day, Jesus Chapel at Pear Tree Green was consecrated.

This was a new chapel built within the parish of St Mary's and was on the far side of the River Itchen. Prior to this, weather and tides had often made crossing the river dangerous for parishioners: it was not always possible to return the same day; the sick and dying did not always have the solace of a minister if he could not cross the water; marriages could not take place; and babies had to be baptised at home. The problem with burials was worse; either the corpse lay unburied for many days, or was dangerously taken across the river with few mourners, which was not considered respectful. The new chapel was consecrated by Bishop Lancelot Andrewes of Winchester, with a form of service which has remained the standard. Previously there had not been a set format for consecration. After the Reformation, new churches and chapels were often subjected to ceremonies little short of 'hocus pocus', and bishops improvised their own rituals, sometimes limiting their ceremony to marking a few Greek characters on the floor of the building. Jesus Chapel was the first to be consecrated by the new service, which was ultimately published in 1659. (A. Spicer, 'God Will Have a House: Defining Sacred Space and Rites of Consecration in Early Seventeenth-Century England', *Defining the Holy*, Spicer and Hamilton (eds), Ashgate, Aldershot, 2005; http://justus.anglican.org/resources/bcp/Andrewes_Consecration_Church.htm)

SEPTEMBER 18TH

1563: On this day, a painter's wife from East Street was employed to paint crosses on the doors of the houses where the plague was present.

Anyone from the house going into the town had to carry a white plague wand, so that people could avoid them. Later outbreaks would see the houses sealed up with the healthy entombed with the sick and dead. Temporary plague booths were built on the town fields. The town carpenters had to supply wood and nails on a 'sale or return' basis. At the end of the outbreak, they were expected to take all materials back. Meanwhile, the town employed six 'bearers and keepers' for the sick. Their duties were to carry the sick to the booths, where they were locked in. Ostensibly they were cared for here, but it is more likely that they were just shut in until they died (or perhaps recovered), when their bodies were borne to the allocated burial site. The bearers and keepers were paid 1s a week and these payments continued until at least the end of the year, which is an indication of the severity of the outbreak. (J.S. Davies, *A History of Southampton*, Southampton, 1883)

SEPTEMBER 19TH

1919: On this day, 170 boys embarked on the 8.50 a.m. train at Millbrook station, and disembarked at Lyndhurst Road station.

Freemantle Church of England Boys' School pupils were on their annual New Forest ramble. From here they walked to Highland Water, the Knightwood Oak, Rhinefield Drive, back to part of Highland Water, Gretnam Wood and the Bombing Camp at Beaulieu Road, before returning to Lyndhurst Road station and back to Millbrook by 5.40 p.m. – having walked a total of 15 miles. The entry in the school log proudly remarked, 'The boys are very keen and walked splendidly, none of them dropping out.' Perhaps they were terrified of being left behind! (M. South, *Titanic Threads*, Eastleigh, 2012, p.121)

September 20th

1586: On this day, Chidiock Tichborne of Southampton was executed at Tyburn in London.

Born in 1558 and brought up by his Catholic family in the town, both he and his father, Peter Tichborne, were arrested by the authorities more than once for their 'popish practices' concerning the use of various religious relics: a practice disapproved of in Elizabeth's Protestant England. In June 1586, Chidiock Tichborne became involved in the Babington Plot, which planned to murder Elizabeth and replace her with her cousin, the Catholic Mary Queen of Scots. The plot was discovered and the conspirators were arrested, tried and sentenced to be hanged, drawn and quartered. The night before his execution, Chidiock wrote a remarkable poem for his wife Agnes. Known as Tichborne's Elegy, the poem has become part of the present-day GCSE syllabus. (Richard Hirsch, 'The Works of Chidiock Tichborne', 1986, *English Literary Renaissance*, 1986, Vol. 16, pp.303-18; 1987, Vol. 17, pp.276-7; Dictionary of National Biography online)

SEPTEMBER 21ST

1603: On this day, Don Juan de Taxis, Spanish Ambassador, had been entertained with bull-baiting at Southampton 'and took great pleasure therein'.

Driven from Oxford due to the severity of the plague there, King James I had advised de Taxis that Southampton was 'one of the healthiest and sweetest towns in his Kingdom'. The Ambassador arrived with fifteen 'gentlemen of quality' and about 140 others. The correspondent, Sir Lewis Lewkenor, the King's Master of Ceremonies, records that they were 'gently received and commodiously lodged'. While they were waiting for Sir Robert Cecil to visit the Ambassador, de Taxis was entertained not only with bull-baiting, but also with music and dancing. No less a person than Lady Lambert had led him into the dance. In return, he had thrown a banquet at his lodgings for many gentlemen and gentlewomen. While de Taxis was here, he also granted certain trade licences to a number of local merchants. His chaplain, however, nearly caused a riot by baptising a boy according to the Roman Catholic rite. As a result, a large number of townspeople gathered outside the Ambassador's lodgings, threatening him and the chaplain with violence. (J. Horrocks, *Assembly Books of Southampton, Vol. I, 1602-1608*, Southampton, 1917, p.xxii; Cal. State Papers Dom. James I, iii, Parts lxxvi and lxxx)

SEPTEMBER 22ND

1849: On this day, the Russian warship *Kamtschatka* arrived in Southampton on her return journey from Madeira.

The ship had also called in on her way out to Madeira, and both visits had been lucrative for the town. Large amounts of ship's stores had been taken on board and the crew had spent considerable time and money buying clothing, cutlery and domestic wares. The officers were polite and disciplined, allowing Sotonians to visit and inspect their very fine ship. However, cleanliness and orderliness were not as good as on an English man-o-war. This was especially noticeable in the manner of feeding the seamen. A large wooden trough was filled with a sort of porridge made from ground beans and a fatty material, which was stirred by two men using rakes. This was served to the seamen in basins and they ate with gusto, using wooden spoons while squatting on their haunches. The captain spoke fluent English and, posing as an American, had visited the Sun Tavern to discover what opinions the locals had of Russians. He apparently heard some very unflattering remarks about the Emperor and his conduct towards Hungary. (*Freeman's Journal & Daily Commercial Advertiser*)

September 23rd

1902: On this day, ratepayers met at the Philharmonic Hall to complain about the smell and appearance of the Western Shore.

Mr White, proprietor of the Central Hotel at the bottom of Bargate Street, said that the smell was very damaging to his business and visitors either cancelled their booking on arrival or departed very soon afterwards. Other lodging houses made similar complaints, and householders said it was impossible to sit in their own sitting rooms due to the odour. The former Mayor, Sir Frederick Perkins, added his voice to the chorus. Complaints had been presented for over two years, but nothing had been done. Someone remarked that he would be in the cemetery before any progress was made, and a heckler called out, 'It has sent some there already!' The matter had been a longstanding annoyance to the community, having been first mentioned back in 1848. A resolution was passed to form a committee to thoroughly investigate the matter and improve things before the next election in November. (*Southern Daily Echo*, 23 September 1902)

September 24th

1785: On this day, William Cowper wrote to his friend, John Newton, about his experience of Southampton:

> I am sorry that an excursion … was attended with so great a drawback upon its pleasures as Miss Cunningham's illness must have been. Had she been able to bathe in the sea, it might have been of service to her; but I knew her weakness and delicacy of habit to be such as did not encourage any hopes that the regimen would suit her. I remember Southampton well, having spent much time there; but though I was young, and had no objections on the score of conscience either to dancing or to cards, I never was in the assembly-room in my life. … A walk to Netley Abbey, or to Freemantle, or to Redbridge, or a book by the fireside, always had more charms for me than any other amusement that the place afforded.

Cowper continues by discussing his dislike of sailing, another pastime for some visitors to Southampton. Later, Cowper and Newton published a book of hymns, including Newton's 'Amazing Grace'. (E.V. Lucas, *William Cowper's Letters: A Selection*, Oxford, 1924)

SEPTEMBER 25TH

1830: On this day, a steam carriage manufactured by Ogle and Summers in their Millbrook foundry, at the bottom of Foundry Lane, was tested.

This was the first steam vehicle capable of travelling along roads and carrying passengers. The vehicle comprised a boiler and steam-engine waggon, pulling a trailer/carriage with twenty passengers. Its speed was estimated at 10mph and it travelled to Eling. The trial attracted crowds eager to see this new type of road transport. Some attempted to follow the carriage, but although horse riders managed to keep up, pedestrians were quickly left behind. Later, Ogle intended to travel to Edinburgh via Birmingham, hoping to achieve 30mph on the way. Engineering reports praised the new invention and stressed its ability to cope with gradients in the roads while carrying large numbers of passengers. One report even went so far as to say, 'This experiment is one of great importance and calls the proprietors of the newly projected railways to pause before they proceed.' With the benefit of hindsight, this seems to have been a very prescient comment. (*The Repertory of Patent Inventions: And Other Discoveries and Improvements*, No. 83, January 1832, p.403; *Hampshire Telegraph*, 27 September 1830)

SEPTEMBER 26TH

1622: On this day, John Webb admitted to being involved in a mass breakout from the gaol in the Bargate.

The men, who were all shackled with leg irons, used a makeshift file made of two knives bound together, sawed through the links, and then knocked the irons off with a hammer. Apparently, searching the prisoners for weapons was not considered necessary! Andrew Stooke filed off the lock of the inner prison door and they all went in. Then Stooke knocked out two of the iron bars which were in place in the loft of the inner prison. They climbed out through the loft, which took them into the main Town Hall and jury room. It was now an easy matter to leave the Bargate via the steps down to the High Street. Some made their escape across the gardens, others left the town through the Bargate itself, and another group – including Webb and Stooke – left the town through the Eastgate. Stooke seems to have been a man of some initiative, because he had the presence of mind to take one of the iron bars with him, and sold it to help him along the way. (R. Anderson, *Examinations and Depositions 1622-1644, Vol. I*, Southampton, 1929, p.3)

September 27th

1615: On this day George Gollop, the Sheriff, was brought before the house and reprimanded for neither owning, nor wearing, a scarlet gown on official occasions, as was required by 'ancient custom'.

The Assembly was very conscious of its dignity, and the scarlet robes had been required dress for its members, officials and their wives for centuries. Gollop never did wear a red gown, preferring to pay the hefty fine of £10 – half of which was immediately returned to him. Whether he got one later on is not recorded, but the town was happy to have him for Mayor in 1621 and again ten years later. Moreover, he served as the town's representative in Charles I's Parliament, so it has to be presumed that he did eventually get a red gown made to uphold the town's dignity. He may not have entirely forgotten the affair; in his will, he set up a charity to provide four men and four women with a gown each year, but he stipulated that it should be 'of some sad colour'. (J. Horrocks, *Assembly Books of Southampton, Vol. IV, 1615-1616*, Southampton, 1925, pp.xxi, 60-1)

September 28th

2011: On this day the annual Brambles Bank cricket match between the Royal Southern Yacht Club, from Hamble, and the Island Sailing Club, from Cowes, took place in the Solent, at approximately 5.45 p.m.

The venue is always the same, but the date and time are reliant on the tides and weather. Brambles Bank is a notorious sandbank in the Solent's busy shipping lane; however, once a year, during extreme low tides, it becomes uncovered for an hour – just long enough for about eight overs of cricket. Small boats carrying the teams (in full cricketing whites), equipment and spectators, gather around the Brambles Bank until the cry 'Tide's Out!' goes up. The wicket is set, scoreboard erected and equipment checked (some years there was even a bar), and the game gets underway. Fielders are often ably assisted by a couple of spaniels and, towards the end of the game, when players find themselves laboriously wading through the waves of the returning tide, the ball is unaccountably thrown further out to sea for the 'fielders' to retrieve. In a game with few rules (if any), one thing is always certain – the teams take it in turns to win, treating the losing team to a well-earned meal afterwards. (The sailing clubs' websites)

SEPTEMBER 29TH

1496: On this day, the wages of various trades and labourers were confirmed.

Annual finances were calculated from four main dates in the calendar: Lady Day, 25 March; Feast of St John the Baptist, 24 June; Michaelmas, 29 September; Christmas, 25 December. On this occasion, Michaelmas was used for the yearly rates of pay to begin. These rates included husbandmen (fieldworkers) to receive 26s 7d; carters and shepherds to receive £1.00; no woman servant to be paid more than 10s annually; no child under the age of fourteen to be paid more than 6s 8d. Each worker also had an annual allowance for clothing, food and drink, although this was never more than 5s. The more seasonal building trades had their rates fixed between Easter and Michaelmas, on a daily basis. Masons, master carpenters, brick layers, tilers, plumbers and joiners were to be paid sixpence without sustenance, but fourpence with food and drink. Hours of work during the summer were from 5 a.m. until 7 p.m. or 8 p.m. This included half an hour for breakfast and an hour and a half for dinner, but the longer dinner break did include half an hour's sleep! (H. Gidden, *The Letters Patent of Southampton, 1415-1612, Vol. II*, Southampton, 1919, pp.79-81)

SEPTEMBER 30TH

1911: On this day, a recent report by the Hampshire Field Club revealed how a local businessman, Henry Huttoft, had hoped to get himself a splendid home when Henry VIII began disposing of the religious houses.

He sent a letter, dated 26 March 1536, to Thomas Cromwell (who was overseeing the Dissolution of the Monasteries) making the following request as a postscript to the main business of the letter: 'There is much talk here about the suppression of religious houses. Let me be a suiter for one viz; the house of Mottisfont, where there is a good friend of mine as good a master and convent as in the country. If none are to be reserved but all are to pass one way, please to let me have it towards my poor living.' 'Poor living' hardly seems applicable to his status, as he was reputed to be one of the wealthiest men in the town. Needless to say, he was unsuccessful and Mottisfont went to a much more important person, William Lord Sandys from the Vine. Henry Huttoft continued living at Bull Hall, opposite the present-day Duke of Wellington public house. (*Hampshire Independent*)

OCTOBER 1ST

1605: On this day Southampton Assembly was concerned about fifty stranded and destitute Irish soldiers.

They had arrived from Cornwall, looking for a ship which should have taken them to Flushing in Holland. It appears they had literally 'missed the boat' and the prevailing winds meant they would be unable to get another ship for several days. The officer in charge, Lieutenant Tirrell, who was under orders from Captain William Darsie, asked the local authorities for lodgings in the town until they could get a ship to Holland. This particular group of Irish soldiers were part of a government scheme to remove some of the more unruly elements from Ireland and send them to Holland to fight in the wars there. Captain Darsie and two others had been given permission to go to Ireland and raise 200 volunteers each to take to the Low Countries. The stranded group had sailed from Ireland, arrived in St Ives, and then marched to Southampton to board a ship. The local authorities, fearful of unrest, moved them on by paying them £2 to go to London. The soldiers are recorded in army reports as arriving late in Holland. (J. Horrocks, *Assembly Books of Southampton, Vol I, 1602-1608*, Southampton, 1917, p.38)

October 2nd

1809: On this day it was advertised that Sarah Siddons, the great tragedienne, would be giving four performances at the Southampton theatre.

Covent Garden theatre, in London, had burned down the previous year and reopened on 18 September, with Mrs Siddons as Lady Macbeth. The new building had a loan to repay and the manager, John Kemble (Sarah's brother), increased ticket prices by 1s. The customers did not like this and there was a riot; the performance stopped and the Riot Act was read from the stage. Violence continued at every performance. Kemble's home was attacked and they kept ladders by the upstairs windows as an escape route. He eventually closed the theatre on 30 September. Presumably Mrs Siddons knew in advance that Kemble would close the theatre if necessary, and sought refuge with her friend Mrs Fitzhugh, at Banister Park in Southampton. At the same time, she agreed to perform in the town. Her first appearance would be as Mrs Beverley in *The Gamester*, on 4 October. The London riots continued for three months and she made few appearances there; she had virtually ended her association with London, preferring to perform in the provinces until her retirement in 1812. (*Hampshire Chronicle*, 2 October 1809; R. Maxwell, *Sarah Siddons*, London, 1970)

OCTOBER 3RD

1844: On this day, the last day of the Southampton cricket season, a novel cricket match took place in front of a large crowd at Day's Ground. The Jury's Inn Hotel now stands on the site.

The Gentlemen of the South Hampshire Club, using a bowling machine (the Catapulta), took on the County Players. It was the first (and probably the last) time in the locality when 'the splendid bowling machine was used'. It had been designed around 1837 by inventor, writer and cricketer Nicholas Wanostrocht ('Felix'), based on the Roman ballista design. Having won the toss, the Gentlemen elected to bat first, and were all out for thirty-nine. Even against the machine, the Players managed to get twenty-one runs in their first innings, with wickets in hand. The Gentlemen's second innings took them to fifty-seven in total, leaving the Players with thirty-seven to win. Luckily, perhaps, for the Gentlemen, darkness stopped play and the match was a draw. A later cricketing experiment in the New Forest was not so well received. Two teams of lady cricketers played a match at Ringwood in 1850. The report said: 'The scene was a disgusting one and altogether discreditable to the district.' (*Hampshire Independent*, 5 October 1844; N. Gannaway, *A History of Cricket in Hampshire*, Hampshire, 1990, pp.27, 29)

OCTOBER 4TH

1338: On this day the town was sacked by French and Genoese raiders.

At 9 a.m. on a Sunday morning, with most of the townspeople at Mass, fifty armed galleys landed on the seafront. From here, the raiders entered the town, murdering the men, violating the women, and reputedly entering St Michael's Church and slaying the congregation, ignoring the tradition of sanctuary which usually applied to those in a church. Then, setting fire to the town and laden with their loot, they disappeared on the next tide. John Stow, the sixteenth-century antiquarian, adds an extra detail to the event: one of the Frenchmen was brought down by a local fieldworker, whereupon the raider cried Rançon. But the English man, not understanding either the language or the rules of war (where ransoms were paid to release prisoners), continued to beat the captive to death, saying, 'Yea, I know well enough thou art a Françon, and therefore shalt thou die!' (C. Platt, *Medieval Southampton, London and Southampton*, 1973, p.109)

OCTOBER 5TH

1992: On this day it was reported that, over the previous weekend, the grave of the comedian Benny Hill had been desecrated and his coffin dug up.

Originally born in Southampton, on 21 January 1924, he was christened Alfred Hawthorne Hill and adopted the stage name of Benny Hill in recognition of his favourite comedian, Jack Benny. Part of his early life was spent as a milkman in nearby Eastleigh, an experience which inspired his best-known song, 'Ernie (The Fastest Milkman in the West)'. It was, however, his impressions and comic timing which gave him his TV break, and, in 1955, *The Benny Hill Show* was launched. A combination of cheeky humour, impressions and songs made it a hit for forty years, and made him one of the biggest stars on American TV. He also played cameo roles in a variety of films, including *The Italian Job* and *Those Magnificent Men in Their Flying Machines*. He died in Teddington, London, on 20 April 1992 and, as he wished, was buried in Southampton. The desecration of his grave was believed to have been done by thieves, who were hoping to steal the jewellery he was reputed to have been wearing when buried. (*Southern Daily Echo*, 5 October 1992; online biography of Benny Hill.

OCTOBER 6TH

1911: On this day, the British Seafarers' Union (BSU) was formed in Southampton.

It broke away from the National Sailors' and Firemen's Union (NSFU) over disagreements about the conduct of the NSFU officials and Union funds. There was a large NSFU membership in Southampton, which meant a high revenue from membership fees. It was, however, a rule of the Union that local branches should only hold a maximum of £10; during a recent strike, local members had received no financial support from headquarters and had been entirely dependent on their own resources. This was felt to be an injustice and, under the leadership of Tommy Lewis, Southampton branch withheld all local contributions, broke away and reformed itself as the BSU. The new Union drew in not only seamen and firemen, but also stewards, cooks and other victualling staff. In Scotland, the Glasgow members of the NSFU followed Southampton's lead and formed another branch of the BSU. In May 1921, the Maritime Board imposed wage reductions which were resisted by both the BSU and the National Union of Ships' Stewards. Neither union was large enough to influence decisions and, later that year, merged to form the Amalgamated Marine Workers' Union. (BSU website; A. Patterson, *A History of Southampton 1700-1914, Vol. III*, Southampton, 1975, p.128)

OCTOBER 7TH

1808: On this day, Jane Austen reported that there had been a fire in the High Street. It had started at Webbes the pastrycook's, in the back of their house, gutting one room entirely. Jane records the flames as very high, but, because it was a still night, there was no wind to fan them or make them spread. Her account gives a graphic description of the alarm which seized adjacent tradespeople:

> ... the engines were immediately in use and before ten the fire was nearly extinguished, tho' it was twelve before everything was considered safe and a guard was kept the whole night ... the Webbes have lost a great deal ... they had a large stock of valuable china and in order to save it, it was taken from the house and thrown down anywhere. The adjoining house, a toyshop, was almost equally injured and Hibbs, whose house comes next was so scared from his senses that he was giving away all his goods ... to anybody who would take them. The crowd in the High Street was immense ...

(D. Le Faye, *Jane Austen's Letters*, Letter 57, Oxford, 1997)

OCTOBER 8TH

1911: On this day a novel demonstration of cookery was given at the Victoria Rooms, using brown paper bags.

The Victoria Rooms were not strangers to gas cookery. They had held a demonstration of gas cookers some years previously, when the report remarked that the audience held a large number of women. Now the use of gas cookers was widespread and some of the drawbacks were coming to public attention, in particular the difficulties of cleaning the appliance. Paper bag cookery would overcome these difficulties; food was placed inside the bags and then cooked in the oven, with the following advantages: it was economical, food was more appetising, and it was a more convenient method. It also allowed the retention of the food's nutritive qualities; there was no joint shrinkage; no smells; almost no pots or pans for cleaning; no basting; and no contamination between foodstuffs. The paper envelope concentrated the juices and flavour, while the method was adaptable to a wide variety of dishes. Perhaps we should abandon aluminium foil and convert to paper bags – it all sounds very familiar. (*Hampshire Advertiser*, 14 October 1911)

OCTOBER 9TH

1913: On this day *The Aeroplane* magazine published a picture of Lieutenant Bigsworth flying a Borel monoplane on the Solent.

Bigsworth was based on the far side of Southampton Water, at Calshot, and became one of the aviation heroes of the coming war. Among his exploits, he was the first pilot to successfully bomb a Zeppelin at night. Even more breathtaking was his attack on a submarine, while he was reconnoitring the sea off Ostend. Seeing the vessel on the surface, he manoeuvred his plane (Farman F.27) and, despite being under fire from shore batteries and the submarine, came down to 500ft and, after careful alignment, was able to drop his bombs with devastating effect. This was the first ever confirmed airborne 'kill' on a submarine. His medals included DSO and Bar; Companion of the Most Distinguished Order of St Michael and St John; and the Air Force Cross. After the war, Bigsworth spent some time in the Air Ministry and found himself working alongside W.E. Johns, who later wrote a series of books about a fictional, daredevil pilot named Bigglesworth, nicknamed 'Biggles'; or, as one eight year old told his parents, 'I'm reading this book at school about a pilot called Big Les!' (Arthur Wellesley Bigsworth online biography; A. Rance (ed.), *Sea Planes and Flying Boats of the Solent*, Southampton, 1981)

OCTOBER 10TH

1675: On this day Elizabeth Fawkens was appointed cowherd for the town, in the place of her dead husband.

The Fawkens family held the position for over 100 years and four generations, from 1644 (when Elizabeth's husband was appointed) until 1763. Moreover, she was not the only woman to hold the post; her grandson's widow also took office. It was not unusual for widows to replace their dead husbands and follow his trade. What is surprising is the continuity of the profession within the Fawkens family for so long. The cowherd was a full-time official, responsible for the management of the Common and care of the householders' cattle. Elizabeth collected the householders' milking cows (already milked), other cattle, and horses early in the morning from outside the Bargate. She called for them either by shouting or using a horn, then drove them onto the Common or other town common lands. The animals were watched over throughout the day, before being returned in the evening. For this service the cowherd was paid tuppence per animal per week. After the death of the last Fawkens, the role of cowherd changed rapidly. Unable to survive on the traditional income, the new cowherd sold beer from his house. The Cowherd's Inn is still a convivial meeting place on the Common. (*Southampton Common*, Southampton, 1979)

OCTOBER 11TH

2010: On this day, at Southampton, Queen Elizabeth II named a ship the *Queen Elizabeth*. It was the third liner to take this name.

Although the ship had been built in Italy, Southampton was to be her home port and, after her naming ceremony, she immediately sailed for her first cruise, to the Canary Islands. Her internal art deco design matched her running partner, the *Queen Victoria*, which was launched in 2007, and harked back to the heyday of the great Cunard liners of the 1930s. Each of the three *Queen Elizabeth* liners had been named by their royal namesake. The first had been launched by Queen Elizabeth (later to become the Queen Mother) in 1938, watched by her twelve-year-old daughter, Princess Elizabeth; later, when the princess had become Queen Elizabeth II, she launched the second ship called *Queen Elizabeth* in 1967. The liner became known as the *QE2*. Now, Queen Elizabeth II has been involved in the launching and naming of three ships carrying her own royal name. (BBC News, broadcast 11 October 2010. Online archive)

OCTOBER 12TH

1838: On this day the foundation stone for the docks was laid. It was preceded by a service at All Saints' Church and a procession down through the town to the designated site.

Work started in earnest the following summer, and, before the first dock was completed, there were 1,600 navvies working on the site. The first dock was officially opened on 29 August 1842. The future of the new facilities was quickly seen to lie in the fast-developing steamships (which could carry passengers) and the highly profitable government-subsidised mail routes. At the time, Falmouth and Dartmouth were the favoured mail ports but, after a strenuous campaign, Southampton won the day and was chosen in preference to Falmouth as the principal packet station. The Royal Mail Line thus moved to Southampton. This was in direct opposition to the Admiralty, who thought the mail was better served from the West Country naval ports. Royal Mail, however, considered that passengers would prefer 'a quiet port far from the bustle of the great naval stations', and so Southampton became a passenger port and home to the great liners. (A. Rance, *Southampton: An Illustrated History*, Southampton, 1980, pp.104-5)

OCTOBER 13TH

1764: On this day Thomas Gray, the poet, wrote to James Brown from Southampton. His letter records his views about the deficiency of the facilities available to genteel visitors in the town:

> This place is still full of Bathers! I know not a soul, nor have been once at the rooms [the Long Rooms were the centre for social life]. The walks all round it are delicious, and so is the weather. Lodgings very dear and fish very cheap. Here is no coffee-house, no bookseller, no pastrycook ... So I proceed to tell you that my health is much improved by the sea; not that I drank it, or bathed in it, as the common people do: no! I only walked by it and looked upon it. The climate is remarkably mild, even in October and November. No snow has been seen to lie here for these thirty years past, the myrtles grow in the ground against the houses, and Guernsey-Lillies bloom in every window.

(T. Gray to James Brown, 13 October 1764, Letter 393, *The Correspondence of Thomas Gray: Volume II: 1756-1765*, Paget Toynbee & Leonard Whibley (eds), Oxford, Oxford University Press, 1935)

October 14th

1556: On this day Nicholas Fuller was baptised at St Michael's Church.

Nicholas studied at King Edward VI Grammar School, when it was situated in God's House loft. Like most schoolboys, he had his favourite lessons and neglected the other subjects. Fascinated by the biblical languages of Hebrew, Syriac, Arabic and Aramaic, Nicholas ultimately devoted his life to their study, and worked to translate biblical texts more accurately. He financed himself at Oxford by becoming tutor to two undergraduates from Southampton. By rising early and working for his own degree, tutoring the two students during the day and studying until late at night, Nicholas gained both his BA and his MA. After taking Holy Orders, he accepted a small country parish with few demands on his time, and devoted his time to study. Nicholas's knowledge was internationally respected and he advised scholars involved with the new King James Bible text. His understanding of Semitic languages influenced many scholars. Nicholas's ambition was to increase the understanding of the Christian text for future generations, and this he surely achieved. (St Michael's parish registers; C.F. Russell, *The History of King Edward VI School*, Southampton, privately published, 1940)

OCTOBER 15TH

1862: On this day the Hartley Institute, forerunner of Southampton University, was opened by the Prime Minister, Lord Palmerston.

The Institute was the result of a legacy left to the town by the eccentric Henry Robinson Hartley. He was born in Southampton, the son of a wealthy wine merchant and ex-Mayor. Immediately after coming in to his wealth, he closed up the family house and never returned. Instead he moved to France, dying at Calais in 1850. In his will he left the majority of his fortune to Southampton, but this was contested by family members. A long court case ensued, vindicating the town's claim but costing half the estate. Nonetheless, the Corporation persevered and, after consultations with local people, a plan was devised to address Hartley's wish for a place of learning for the town. Lord Palmerston laid the foundation stone in 1860 and, amid great excitement, opened the Institute two years later. So great was the enthusiasm that some members of the public climbed up the outside of Holy Rood Church to get a view. Unfortunately, someone dislodged a piece of masonry and it crashed to the ground, amidst the throng below. Miraculously, it missed striking anyone. A brass cross in the pavement commemorates the event. (J.S. Davies, *A History of Southampton*, Southampton, 1883, pp.127-31)

OCTOBER 16TH

1909: On this day, the 'Flora' controversy hit the headlines.

The art world had been surprised by the discovery of a new Leonardo da Vinci work, 'undoubtedly' dating from around 1500. Initially sold in Southampton for a few pounds, it was then sold for £150. The new owner offered it to the British Museum, who declined. The Kaiser Friedrich Museum, in Berlin, then bought it as a Leonardo. However, Southampton antiquary Mr C.F. Cooksey, who had sold the wax bust, alerted the *Illustrated London News* to his doubts. They ran the story for several weeks with comparative photographs of the 'Flora' bust in Berlin (which had been declared genuine by the Kaiser himself) and photographs taken years before in Richard Cockle Lucas's studio in Southampton. Lucas was an expert wax sculptor – arguably this was his best medium; he also (as did other sculptors) frequently stuffed his work with old newspapers or material. On one occasion he used an old waistcoat. He also liked to mimic the styles of other artists for his own amusement. 'Flora' was ultimately found to be stuffed with part of a nineteenth-century quilt and removed from display. (*Illustrated London News*, 16 October 1909)

OCTOBER 17TH

1772: On this day the trial of John Fieldhouse was reported. Fieldhouse was an army officer who had attempted 'to commit a detestable crime on a lad of this town'.

Although Southampton was not unfamiliar with homosexual activity, it did react strongly to visitors or newcomers making advances towards local boys. Fieldhouse had come to public attention the previous July, when a letter was sent to the *General Evening Post* complaining that 'the vice which was the talk of London' had appeared in Southampton. The outrage was sparked by a case where the offender, Captain Jones, had received a Royal Pardon and reprieve from execution. Sodomy was a capital offence because it deprived the Crown of new manpower for military service, and was therefore viewed as treason. Rumours about Fieldhouse had begun to circulate and, when he attended a ball, he was asked to leave. He fled back to his rooms, where the constables came to arrest him. He was caught when he got stuck trying to escape through the garret window. The locals reacted violently, making an effigy of Fieldhouse in the pillory and burning it. Bearing this reaction in mind, judgement on Fieldhouse was limited to a heavy fine and six months in gaol. (M. South, 'Homophobia in Eighteenth-Century Southampton', *Hampshire Studies*, 2011, pp.207-20)

OCTOBER 18TH

1784: On this day, Jean-Pierre Blanchard's hydrogen balloon landed at Romsey. When he touched down Blanchard released a carrier pigeon which only flew about 4 miles to Chilworth, just outside Southampton. At this point the pigeon either lost interest, or was seduced by one of the pigeons at a local farmhouse and decided to move in there, instead of continuing its journey home to London.

Blanchard had moved to London in August 1784, where he took part in a number of successful flights across the Home Counties. The naturalist Gilbert White recorded Blanchard's balloon 'migrating' overhead at Selborne. The Frenchman had made his first ascents in France earlier the same year, but believed he could get better scientific support in England. He was determined to acquire as much scientific data as possible on his flights, measuring wind speed, air currents and temperature. He was particularly interested in navigating his balloons – trying oar systems, flapping wings, and, more usefully, a hand-cranked windmill/propeller. They all proved ineffective, but nonetheless the balloon flew some 115km from the military academy in Chelsea, to land in Romsey. (*Whitehall Evening Post*, 23 October 1784; R. Holmes, *The Age of Wonder*, London, 2008, pp.145-54)

OCTOBER 19TH

1856: On this day the steamship *Oneida* set sail from Southampton to Australia on the inaugural sailing trip for the European & Australian Royal Mail Co. Ltd.

The ship was a year old, previously having been requisitioned and used to take troops to the Crimea. Returned to civilian service, her owners proclaimed they were very pleased with the docks at Southampton. On 16 October 1856, the Mayor, Richard Andrews, gave a dinner at the Dolphin to mark the inaugural journey. Three days later the *Oneida* set sail, reaching Melbourne on 23 December 1856. On board she had sixty passengers, including Sir Henry Barkly, the incoming Governor of Victoria. Her arrival was celebrated in Australia and a new dance, the Oneida Polka, was composed in her honour. This was during the Australian gold rush, and she started the return voyage in January, with seventy passengers and 10,000oz of gold on board. Unfortunately, she suffered a major breakdown and, with delays for repairs and bad weather, did not reach Southampton until August – with two extra passengers. There had been two births on the voyage. (*See* December 6th) (J. Watts, 'What's in a Name?', Friends of Southampton Old Cemetery Newsletter, No. 31)

October 20th

1987: On this day, the damage done by the hurricane (more correctly called a storm) on the night of 15/16 October was being assessed.

Thousands of trees had been lost across Hampshire; Shanklin's historic pier on the Isle of Wight had been entirely destroyed; and 30,000 homes were without electricity due to damaged power lines. Miles of cabling needed to be replaced and local cable-producing firms were working around the clock to meet demand. Workers reported working for forty-eight hours before finally going home to bed. Masses of frozen food was defrosting in domestic freezers and would probably have to be thrown away. At Hamble, an attempt would be made at high tide to refloat the grounded cargo vessel *Sam G*. (*Southern Daily Echo*)

OCTOBER 21ST

1769: On this day, for the benefit of visitors to the town, it was decided to improve the amenities of the seaside walk called the Platform. The amount set aside for the work was £40, which was intended to repair and beautify the walk. Many visitors were more than happy with the town already. William Cowper, the poet, wrote that:

> The sun shone bright upon the sea, and the country on the border was the most beautiful I had ever seen. We sat down at the end of an eminence at the end of the arm of the sea which runs between Southampton and the New Forest. Here it was on a sudden as if another sun had been kindled that instant in the heavens on purpose to dispel sorrow and vexation of spirit. I felt the weight of all my misery taken off and my heart became light and joyful in a moment.

(E. Aubrey, *Speed's History of Southampton*, Southampton Record Society, Southampton, 1909, p.vii)

OCTOBER 22ND

1921: On this day, the mystery of the disappearing cat was solved.

A local man, who preferred to remain anonymous, had an elderly cat which he decided was getting too old to stay out at night. The pet was carefully shut in the kitchen each evening, but every morning it was outside the back door waiting to be let in. The man was accused of carelessness and not making sure the kitchen was secure, but, despite his best efforts, the cat still appeared outside every morning. Then, one moonlit night, being unable to sleep, the man got up and went outside to look at the starlit sky. After a few minutes he became aware of feline noises apparently coming from the heavens themselves and, gazing upwards towards the sound, was astonished to see his cat's head and two front paws appear out of the top of his chimney, shortly followed by the rest of the animal. Elderly or not, the cat was allowed to stay outside in the future. (*Southern Daily Echo*, 24 October 1921)

OCTOBER 23RD

1851: On this day the Hungarian freedom fighter, Lajos Kossuth, landed at Southampton at the start of a three-week visit to the UK.

He was famous not only as a lawyer, journalist and politician, but also as the Regent-President of Hungary – a title he had invented in an attempt to lessen the differences between Royalist and Republican factions. His activities for the promotion of liberal views had landed him in prison for four years, and during this time he had learned English by reading the Bible and Shakespeare. A report on his speeches in England said his language was 'wonderfully archaic and theatrical', but very clear. When Kossuth arrived in Southampton he was a fugitive, but was regarded as a hero and given a suitable welcome wherever he went. Richard Andrews, the Southampton Lord Mayor, gave an address, and thousands gathered to cheer the visitor and present him with a flag of the Hungarian Republic. From the UK Kossuth went to America, where his reception was described as 'equally enthusiastic if less dignified'. (*Encyclopaedia Britannica*; *Manchester Times*, 12 November 1851)

OCTOBER 24TH

1617: On this day, Alderman Philip Toldervey's wife was threatened with prison.

Toldervey had been Mayor in 1609-1610, but his wife had been 'visited with a kind of lunacy'. She disturbed people in their houses, used unfit behaviour in church, and her speeches were 'many times idle, odious and most scandalous against his Majesty and the state'. Her behaviour was dangerous not only to herself but to others. Her neighbours went in fear of her and, two years before, in October 1615, Philip had been requested to restrain her and keep her indoors until she regained her senses. In 1617 the matter was still unresolved and the Assembly members called Philip to account again. Things were getting ugly. He was reminded that 'four of the members have paid for the boards and nails and the workman to make a safe and secure place to keep her … but she is still loose. Her behaviour is a disgrace to the town, especially for the wife of one of the Assembly. If she is not kept in, she will be sent to prison until we can be certain of her good behaviour'. The result is not known. (J. Horrocks, *Assembly Books of Southampton, Vol. IV, 1615-1616*, Southampton, 1925, pp.xx-xi, 30, 43; Assembly Book minutes SC2/1/6, 1602-42)

OCTOBER 25TH

1784: On this day the Mayor was held up by a highwayman on the Common, near the Cowherd's Inn.

The Mayor, John Monckton, was driving himself and his daughter back from South Stoneham at 4 p.m. when they were stopped by a highwayman and robbed of a watch and money. Monckton described the thief as wearing a red waistcoat, beige coat and riding 'a very bad horse'. This particular stretch of road across the Common could almost be compared to Hampstead Heath due to the frequency of the robberies. A coach coming into the town had been stopped by a highwayman in 1775. The robber had then robbed a local inhabitant at the same spot a short while later. On this occasion, however, the victim apparently recognised the thief, who returned the stolen goods and begged not to be described because he was the sole supporter of a wife and large family. Although the incident was reported, no identification was given in the newspaper, so maybe the victim did take pity on the would-be thief. (*Hampshire Chronicle*, 27 November 1775; 25 October 1784; A. Patterson, *A History of Southampton 1700-1914, Vol. I*, Southampton, 1966, pp.43, 50)

OCTOBER 26TH

1771: On this day, Mrs Orlebar returned to London after spending several weeks enjoying the delights of the Southampton Spa.

Mrs Orlebar, gossip and socialite, reported on the fashionable events in Southampton during 'the season'. The town was renowned for its sea-bathing facilities and she records in detail the whole procedure when her sister-in-law 'took the flounce', as the ritual was called. Female bathers were given long, green flannel gowns and socks to wear; they tucked their hair into a leather bag, and their precious front curls were protected by an oiled silk band. Bathing took place at Mrs Martin's tidal baths under the supervision of a female attendant, Mrs Tring, who gave encouragement to each participant. Mrs Orlebar's description of her first experience is similar to many people's early swimming lessons: 'A panic struck me, but I gave my hands to Mrs Tring and took the Flounce, which for the moment was the most wonderful sensation! I rose above the water near strangled by the quantity (by not shutting my mouth) I had inadvertently swallowed. How happy did I feel myself when on dry ground again!' (R. Douch, *Visitors' Descriptions of Southampton, 1540-1956*, Southampton, 1978, pp.16-18)

OCTOBER 27TH

1877: On this day, the Annual General Meeting of the Southampton Industrial Ragged School was held.

It was reported that the daytime teaching of the boys would now be taken over by the School Board, which was in a better financial situation than the subscribers to provide teachers for the boys. The evening and weekend activities would be for religious and moral training, and would still take place at the Palk Memorial Hall in St George's Road, Houndwell. The Chairman was glad to report that Miss Palk still took an interest in the activities of the organisation. It was hoped that needy boys could be trained to take part in some industrial activities, giving them the opportunity to support themselves. Summarising the achievements of the association, the Chairman said that, during its twenty-nine-year existence, it had taken nearly 3,000 destitute boys off the streets and provided them with an elementary education. For some this was the only education they had known, and the Board could congratulate themselves for rescuing so many young boys from danger and potential lives of crime. (*Hampshire Advertiser*)

OCTOBER 28TH

1893: On this day the Fire Service Committee of the council was called to account for the delays in getting to a fire when called.

The time between receiving the call and arriving at a fire seemed to vary; the fire service estimated that it took between seven and ten minutes, and a council member claimed it was nearer half an hour. Some of the confusion arose because the fire service excluded the time it took to prepare the engine. On average, travelling time took ten to fifteen minutes at the most. Questioning revealed that the delay in preparing the engine was because the horses had to be collected from elsewhere. The question of why they were not kept at the fire station was not satisfactorily answered. An uncomplimentary comparison was drawn with London, where the horses were on site and the engine could be prepared in two and a half minutes. (*Hampshire Advertiser*)

OCTOBER 29TH

1958: On this day two dogs, Flash and Peggy, signed the Mayor's visitors' book with their paw marks.

The two dogs had become a familiar sight around the town, achieving their own minor celebrity status. Flash was a greyhound who had been rescued by his owners, Mr and Mrs Corbin, when they lived in Doncaster. Over the years he had lost his sight and, when his owners moved to Southampton, he was completely disorientated. The Corbins took in another rescue dog, Peggy, and she became Flash's guide dog, leading him around the town. Flash's confidence returned as they walked together; the little mongrel had given the greyhound a new lease of life. When the Mayor heard their story, the Corbins were invited to bring the two dogs to the Civic Centre to meet the Mayor and sign the visitors' book, which they duly did. (*Southern Daily Echo*, 29 October 1958)

OCTOBER 30TH

1847: On this day an extraordinary phenomenon was seen in the evening sky, which appeared to have been something like the aurora borealis.

At 10 p.m. a thin line of vapour was seen stretching upwards from the horizon towards the nearly-full moon. Gradually, more mist gathered on each side of the column, and under the light of the moon it assumed a bright flame colour. Small patches of mist from each side were shooting long streamers of white light into the sky, while the stars continued to shine through the whole phenomenon. The white streamers shifted and changed their positions, but the central red column remained stationary. The display lasted until 10.20, when the red colour faded and the whole took on the appearance of smoke. There was considerable speculation about the cause of the display, which was originally thought to have been caused by a serious fire somewhere – but the phenomenon had been witnessed in Exeter and London as well. There had been a large volcanic eruption earlier that year in the Atlantic, when Fogo had produced lava from seven fissures; perhaps this was the result of some volcanic ash in the atmosphere. (*Hampshire Advertiser & Salisbury Guardian*)

OCTOBER 31ST

1877: On this day there were several cases of fraudulent trading brought before the Police Court.

Anne White, from Bitterne Manor Farm, was convicted of adulterating milk with 19 per cent water; she was fined £1 and costs. Thomas Collins from Kingsland was fined the same amount for having a butter scale which had a piece of metal fixed underneath, weighing against the customer by nearly 1oz. Alfred Frampton, also from Kingsland, had a whole set of defective weights which were confiscated; while Alfred Marshal, a greengrocer in Upper Canal Walk, had two defective weights. William Barrow, a fishmonger in Canal Walk, had light weights too. The size of these weights – 14lb each – must be some indication of the amounts of fish available at that time. (*Hampshire Advertiser*)

———— ◆ ————

1912: On this day a house in Shirley was struck by lightning. A single clap of thunder directly overhead was followed by torrential rain. A large portion of the roof tiles was blasted off and the chimney was split, right the way down, blowing the fireplace and mantelpiece right across the room. (*Southern Echo*)

NOVEMBER 1ST

1888: On this day, William Mineer was brought to the Police Court for begging in Bedford Place.

His wife spoke on his behalf, telling how she had been sick in the Infirmary and was thus unable to work; the previous evening they had had no fire, no food and no money to pay the rent which was due. The prisoner himself told the Bench that he had been a clerk, but sickness and misfortune had incapacitated him. Mr Chipperfield, the Chairman, discharged the prisoner and gave him money to buy the surgical instrument he needed. No indication is given what this might have been – an artificial leg perhaps? (*Southern Daily Echo*)

NOVEMBER 2ND

1865: On this day a new drinking fountain was installed on Asylum Green, at the bottom of the Avenue.

It replaced the old pond and cattle pound, which had become both rundown and insanitary. John Ransom was a local politician and a well-known colourful figure in the town, who enjoyed celebrating his election wins with lavish gestures. The drinking fountain was one such gesture, when he decided to meet 'the needs for a water supply for way-worn cattle and horses' and their equally thirsty owners. The drinking fountain has a bowl on each side and a horse trough next to it. The instruction 'drink but waste not' was carved into the structure as a reminder about abstinence and frugality in all things. After its installation, Ransom provided his fellow councillors and friends to one of his lavish meals, where abstinence and frugality were not on the menu! (A.G.K. Leonard, *More Stories of Southampton Streets*, Southampton, 1989, p.56)

NOVEMBER 3RD

1933: On this day, the Civic Centre Law Courts were opened by the Lord High Chancellor, the Rt Hon. Viscount Sankey.

The Civic Centre project had been proposed in 1924, and a public meeting in January 1925 attracted 2,000 people. Various concerns were raised; one fear, that the building would fall into the old canal tunnel underneath, was groundless. After negotiation between the political parties, the project was agreed and, out of forty-seven plans submitted, E. Berry Webber's design was accepted. The complex comprised four separate but interconnected blocks, and the foundation stone for the project was laid by Prince Albert, later to become King George VI. There had been no tower in the design, but, early in 1930, this was revised. In November 1930 a balloon was flown over the site at the height of the intended clock tower; Councillor Sidney Kimber and Berry Webber drove around to check that the balloon could be seen from vantage points in the town. Eventually everything was completed and, during the Law Courts opening ceremony, the clock tower carillon chimed out Isaac Watts' hymn, 'O God Our Help in Ages Past', over the town for the first time. A Southampton landmark had been born. (A. Rance, *Southampton: An Illustrated History*, Southampton, 1980, pp.149-51)

NOVEMBER 4TH

1928: On this day National Rat Week started, and Highfield Scouts were out helping to kill rats.

The 14th Highfield Scout Troop boasts of being one of the oldest in the world. It was founded in March 1909 by Revd Roach, and still retains its original brown and green scarf colours. Since that time, the troop has served the community in a variety of ways. During the First World War they worked at the rest camp on the Common, with French forces and the wounded. For this service they were awarded the Military Cadet Medal by the French Ministry of Defence. As well as this they were involved with registering aliens, working in the docks, and guarding bridges and other installations. Small wonder, then, that the task of catching rats gave them no fear. National Rat Week had been instigated originally to reduce the rats on agricultural premises, but had become extended to include towns. This was a means of educating the population about the health dangers and nuisance of rats. The event was held annually at the beginning of November, when householders were encouraged to keep a record of how many rats they had killed. To help them, free rat poison was distributed! (Southampton 14th Highfield Scout Troop website, http://www.highfieldscouts.org.uk/?page_id=155)

NOVEMBER 5TH

1873: On this day, Sidney Kimber was born in Southampton. He was destined to become one of the leading figures of the town's political scene.

In 1900 he took over his father's brickyard at Highfield and, ten years later, was elected to the local council, where he quickly began to make an impression. His vision and energy were largely instrumental in building the Civic Centre, which centralised all the different departments of the council; the clock tower was known locally as 'Kimber's Chimney' (*see* November 3rd). Part of the deal when the Civic Centre was built was the provision of 2,000 council houses. Having successfully gained better accommodation for the town officials (and as a result more convenient transport links through the town) and produced new homes for ordinary people, Kimber now turned his attention to the town's leisure facilities. In the Bassett area, between Burgess Road and the Avenue, lies his greatest brainchild – the Sports Centre, containing a golf course, cricket grounds, tennis courts, football pitches, bowling greens and a boating lake. (Ian Broad, *The Illustrated Guide to Southampton*, Southampton, 1982, p.17)

NOVEMBER 6TH

1920: On this day, the Cenotaph was unveiled by Sidney Kimber.

Early in 1919, plans for a permanent memorial to the town's war dead had been discussed and, amongst others, Sir Edwin Lutyens submitted a design. A site at West Marlands (now Watts Park) was made available for the scheme and Lutyens' design was approved by the council. When it was unveiled, there were 1,800 names inscribed into its Portland stone surface. These would be increased to 2,008 eventually. Southampton's Cenotaph proved to be the blueprint when Lutyens was asked to submit a design for the national monument in Whitehall, London. Although slightly simpler, it is easily recognisable as a derivative of Southampton's memorial. Moreover, the design for the altar of remembrance (adjoining the Southampton Cenotaph) was used for the altars in all the war cemeteries in Flanders. The design of Southampton's war memorial is as much a commemoration of the far-sightedness of the councillors, who chose a modern architect for the project, as the many service personnel it honours. (A. Rance, *Southampton: An Illustrated History*, Southampton, 1980, p.143)

NOVEMBER 7TH

1837: On this day there was a terrible fire in a paint store in the High Street. This was owned by Messrs King Witt & Co., who were lead merchants.

As well as paint there were barrels and containers of turpentine and linseed oil, which were in danger of exploding and spreading the flames. At the same time, the lead was melting and dripping down from the upper floor. Passers-by and neighbouring householders tried to prevent the fire from spreading. Twenty-two selfless men entered the blazing building in an attempt to remove some of the inflammable materials before the upper floor collapsed. They all lost their lives, but their aim was achieved – the fire did not spread. The Corporation recognised their heroism and undertook to give their families all necessary assistance. A memorial to their courage, on the outside of Holy Rood Church, records each individual and his age, ranging from George Bell (sixteen) to John Harley (fifty). Using typically Victorian language, the panels tell the story of the men's action and the gratitude of the public who 'erect this grateful but melancholy memorial of their intrepidity, their sufferings and their awfully sudden removal into an eternal state'. (A. Patterson, *A Selection from the Southampton Corporation Journals, 1815-35, and Borough Council Minutes, 1835-47*, Southampton, 1965, p.90)

November 8th

1890: On this day, Mr Bicker-Caarten began his campaign about living conditions for the poor in Southampton. In the first of a series of letters to the press, he described St James' Ward near the docks:

> The district itself, the small, close, dirty and evil-smelling streets, generally blocked up at one end ... the maze of little courts and passages leading out of them, with their wretched tumbledown houses closely packed with human beings, with no provision for decency or cleanliness ... and then the tribes of children, hungry, dirty, barefooted and wild, utterly neglected, growing up to swell the ranks of crime and pauperism ... Then the scenes that occur in these abodes of misery and darkness, the drunkenness, brutality, immorality ... cannot be described ... this district appears to be ... given up as hopeless by Church and State.

A series of letters resulted, both supporting and criticising him, but he maintained his crusade and the cause was taken up by a council member, Edward Gayton. Eventually, the campaigners won and a programme of slum clearance was implemented, culminating in the first council houses being built in the St Michael's area in 1902. (*Southampton Times*, 8 November 1890; A. Patterson, *A History of Southampton 1700-1914, Vol. III*, Southampton, 1975, pp.107-8)

NOVEMBER 9TH

1907: On this day, Southampton Harbour Board issued a stern warning to fishing boats to stop anchoring in the docks, as they were 'rendering navigation extremely difficult to large steamers frequenting the port'. (*Southern Daily Echo*)

◆

1961: On this day, Derek Piggott flew the Southampton University Man-Powered Air Craft (SUMPAC) a distance of 50ft at a height of 6ft off the ground. Pedalling furiously and wearing a yoke attached to the fin to aid stability, Piggott achieved the first man-powered flight in Britain.

The aircraft was designed and built at Southampton University. Construction had begun in January 1961, with a grant of £1,500 from the Royal Aeronautical Society. To maximise the power produced by its 'engine' (Piggott), the aircraft had to be very light (130lb) and produce as much 'lift' as possible. This was achieved with a framework of spruce, balsa and aluminium, covered with clear nylon sheeting and an 8ft propeller. The wingspan was 80ft, with a 25ft-long fuselage. Some minor modifications were made before the second flight in February 1962. On this occasion, the aircraft flew 650 yards at a height of 15ft. The SUMPAC is now on display in the Solent Sky Museum in Southampton. (http://www.spitfireonline.co.uk/popup/other7.html)

NOVEMBER 10TH

1769: On this day, the application for a Paving Act was approved by the local inhabitants. The Corporation drew up its proposals, which would have to be approved by Parliament.

The state of the town's roads were a cause for concern, especially when the fashionable visitors expected better and safer walking and riding conditions. It was reported that one lady had stepped into what seemed to be a shallow puddle, only to find herself in a deep pothole, with water well above her ankles! The new Act enabled a group of Paving Commissioners to be set up to inspect the roads; they would be empowered to fine those who did not carry out the necessary work in front of their houses. Pavements were to be provided, together with lighting; shop fronts were not to encroach upon the pavements, nor were overhanging signs to be too low; and cellar trap doors were to be kept closed when not in use. It appears that it was not unusual for people to fall into the open trap doors! (E. Aubrey (ed.), *Speed's History of Southampton*, Southampton, 1909, pp.xxiv-xxx; J. Stovold, *Minute Book of the Pavement Commissioners for Southampton, 1770-1789*, Southampton Records Series, Vol. 31, Southampton, 1990)

NOVEMBER 11TH

1893: On this day, a memorial stone instead of a foundation stone was laid by Mrs Eliot Yorke, at the building site of the intended emigrant lodging house.

With the arrival of the America Line shipping in the town, the number of emigrants travelling to America had increased considerably. Many came from European cities and frequently needed accommodation before travelling to America; at the present time this was only provided at London. The new lodging house – in Albert Road, and to be suitably named Atlantic Hotel – would comprise four floors, be steam heated, and have bedrooms for up to 350 people: 'bathrooms, lavatories, disinfecting rooms and indeed all the necessary accommodation for emigrants.' Mrs Eliot Yorke, a leading figure in the Temperance Movement, had agreed to lay the foundation stone in July when the building was started, but circumstances had prevented this and the ceremony had been delayed until November. The Mayor, Mr Lemon (*see* September 14th), suggested that it should be called a 'memorial stone' instead. The backgrounds of the VIPs involved (temperance, sanitation and health) surely give some insight into the prevailing attitudes towards the foreign emigrants at that time. (*Hampshire Advertiser*)

NOVEMBER 12TH

1851: On this day, the press in Manchester praised Richard Andrews, the Mayor of Southampton, for his reforming attitudes. The local newspaper also recounted his progress as a self-made man.

Some of the key events of Andrews' life demonstrated his determination to be undeterred by problems. Southampton regarded him as its own Dick Whittington because he had walked from his home at Bishops Sutton to Southampton, for work. Once here he set up his own coach-building factory, and earned an international reputation. The report, however, makes it clear that Dick's walking exploits went further than Southampton. He had been apprenticed to an ironworker and coach-builder in Itchenstoke, walking the 10 miles there and back to Bishops Sutton each day. Towards the end of his time, he met the lady he would marry at a village dance in Tichborne. Unfortunately, she was only visiting and returned to Hounslow, nearly 50 miles away. Dick walked to Tichborne and back several times over the following months, until his apprenticeship was finished. Then he walked to Hounslow, where they were married. A tradition celebrating Hampshire Dick's wedding was maintained in Hounslow for many years, by banging various iron implements in honour of his trade. (*Manchester Times*, 12 November 1851)

NOVEMBER 13TH

1852: On this day the *Hampshire Advertiser* printed the following advertisement:

> Do you want luxuriant and beautiful whiskers?
>
> Many preparations have been introduced to the public but none has gained such a world-wide celebrity and immense sale as Emily Dean's Criniline. It is guaranteed to produce whiskers, eyebrows etc in a few weeks with the utmost certainty; and it will be found eminently successful in nourishing, curling and beautifying the hair, checking and preventing greyness in all its stages; strengthening weak hair, preventing it falling off etc.
>
> For the reproduction of hair in baldness from whatever cause, and at whatever age, it stands unrivalled, never having failed.

———◆———

1963: On this day a very different hair advertisement appeared in the *Southern Daily Echo*:

> Are you a girl who prefers skilful hairstyling with a young approach?
>
> Who enjoys the atmosphere of a small but friendly salon?
>
> Who loves individual attention and service, with a desire to please?
>
> We are young stylists; we believe we are skilful; we love hairdressing; we would be delighted to wait on you.

The approach may have changed but human vanity doesn't.

NOVEMBER 14TH

1952: On this day, Margot Fonteyn returned to her London home on a stretcher, by ambulance.

She was the prima ballerina in the Sadler's Wells Ballet, who were on tour and performing at the Gaumont Theatre (now the Mayflower Theatre). On the first evening she had complained of a sore throat and this was diagnosed initially as tonsillitis. However, it soon became apparent that this was not the case and that she was suffering from something else. More tests revealed that she had a mild form of diphtheria, and she was quickly isolated in a glass cubicle in the fever ward of Southampton's Chest Hospital. The rest of the company had to be tested, the performances cancelled and the theatre fumigated. Fonteyn was not released until there were no signs of the diphtheria bacteria in her nose and throat, which was approximately two weeks later. It was rumoured that the local medical officer of health, Maurice Williams, had some very 'colourful' words to say about the ballet company bringing the disease into the town, as there had not been any cases of diphtheria there for many years. (*Southern Daily Echo*, 14 November, 1952; Dictionary of National Biography online)

NOVEMBER 15TH

1888: On this day, Kate Philp was brought before the Police Court for assaulting her husband.

The couple lodged in Portland Street and the husband had come home to find there was no fire lit, or meal ready, and his wife and child were out. He obtained some hot water from another male lodger and returned to make some tea. His wife returned shortly afterwards and was very annoyed that he had obtained hot water from elsewhere. She put down the child and proceeded to beat Mr Philp about the head with her fists, eventually throwing the teapot at him. Mr Philp said she was drunk at the time, and the neighbour verified that she had recently taken 'to beer'. Both husband and wife agreed that Mr Philp gave Kate all his wages every week, which amounted to 18s. Mr Chipperfield, from the Bench, remarked that there were few husbands in Southampton who did this and she should appreciate it. The case was adjourned for a month. (*Southern Daily Echo*)

NOVEMBER 16TH

1884: On this day, baby Rose Foster was received into the Highfield Church congregation.

Initially this appears to be nothing unusual, but Rose was born with the rare congenital condition of phocomelia, generally described as having limbs like seal's flippers. None of her siblings showed any evidence of the condition. Rose bravely made her way in the world by exhibiting herself in various novelty sideshows, including those run by Barnum & Bailey and the Ringling Brothers. Working in this way, she toured the world and met several European crowned heads, often being described as the 'Eighth Wonder of the World'. Interviewers remarked upon her charming personality and her independence, as she was capable of knitting, writing and attending to most household chores. Being part of the travelling shows, Rose had her own large trailer, where she lived with her husband after her marriage at the age of thirty-four. When she retired from show business Rose returned to live in Southampton with her sister, where she celebrated her seventieth birthday. There is no local record of her death, but this seems to have occurred in the late 1950s. (A.G.K. Leonard, *Journal of the Southampton Local History Forum*, Summer 2007)

NOVEMBER 17TH

1877: On this day, a serious driving offence committed by a lad from Freemantle was brought to court.

A police officer a few miles away, in Totton, had seen John Browne driving a waggon through the village without using the reins. The reins were lying across the horse's back, completely useless. When the policeman stopped him, pointed out the offence and asked his name and age, the boy gave his name as John Browne and said he could drive as well without the reins as with. Tracing the boy proved difficult, but the officer persevered and eventually traced him to Freemantle, discovering that his name was James Trodd, aged fifteen. His father described him as 'only a child'. Nonetheless, 'the child' was fined and told to pay costs. (*Hampshire Advertiser*)

NOVEMBER 18TH

1947: On this day, work on the Concordia aircraft was suspended by the manufacturer, Cunliffe-Owen.

Intended as a short-haul passenger plane, the aircraft was probably produced too soon after the Second World War, during the ongoing austerity throughout Europe. The first flight had taken place at Eastleigh (Southampton) Airport on 19 May 1947, but only two aircraft were eventually completed, despite an extensive European sales tour and campaign. The company had been successful throughout the war, building, repairing and adapting Seafires. It also held, at Eastleigh, the Lancaster bomber adapted as the escape plane for the royal family should the need arise. After the war, the company adapted Lancaster bombers as air-sea rescue planes, carrying rescue dinghies instead of bombs in their bomb bays – the boats were dropped to anyone in the water needing assistance, prior to the arrival of the lifeboat. After the Concordia setback, the company (owned by British-American Tobacco magnate Sir Hugo Cunliffe-Owen) withdrew from aircraft production and reputedly went into heating radiator manufacture instead. (http://www.aviastar.org/air/england/cunliffe-owen_concordia.php; Dictionary of National Biography; P. New, *The Solent Sky*, Southampton, 1976, pp.101-2)

NOVEMBER 19TH

1935: On this day, John Rushworth Jellicoe (Earl Jellicoe and native of Southampton) died.

Born in 1859, Jellicoe had attended the Bannister Court School before joining the Royal Navy in 1872 and training at Dartmouth. Ten years later he took part in the Egyptian War, marching to Cairo. By 1897 he had his own command and was sent to Peking to relieve the legations during the Boxer Rebellion; here, he was badly wounded in the chest. The wound was thought fatal and he made his will – but recovered fully, apart from carrying the bullet lodged in his left lung for the rest of his life. Just before the First World War, he was made Second Sea Lord and took command of the Atlantic Fleet. Returning to the Admiralty under Winston Churchill, who was First Sea Lord at that time, Jellicoe was made Commander of the Grand Fleet. He famously engaged the German fleet at the Battle of Jutland in 1916 and, a year later, was made First Sea Lord. Jellicoe always maintained his links with Southampton, and the flag he flew on his ship at Jutland was presented to Freemantle School, where it hung in one of the classrooms for many years. (Dictionary of National Biography online)

NOVEMBER 20TH

1875: On this day, a number of unburied children were found on Stephen Blundell's premises. Blundell was a local undertaker and he, his wife and a man in Blundell's employment were all sent to the Assizes on charges of clothing theft and receiving money under false pretences. (*Royal Cornwall Gazette*, 20 November 1875)

———•◆•———

1875: On this day, Southampton Council resolved to repair the roads in Bevois Valley; these were in such a poor state that water was unable to flow down the drains properly, and caused flooding in the area. (*See* September 14th) (*Hampshire Advertiser*)

NOVEMBER 21ST

1885: On this day, Southampton Football Club was born.

In about 1881, St Mary's Church had established a club for the choristers, Sunday school teachers, and others who took an active part in parish life. Known as the St Mary's Church of England Young Men's Association, members pursued various activities; 'glee-singing', cricket, athletics and gymnastics were all popular, so it was natural to include football as well. The first match was against Freemantle FC, played on the 'backfield' of the new Hampshire County Cricket Club ground in Northlands Road. St Mary's won 5–1. For the next couple of seasons they played local 'friendlies' on the Common, but in 1887 they joined the Hampshire Football Association. By the end of that season they had changed their name to St Mary's FC, had an enthusiastic group of supporters, had been nicknamed 'the Saints', and won the Hampshire FA Junior Cup. The Saints won the Junior Cup outright in 1890, having achieved wins in two more consecutive finals. The Saints were now established as Southampton's premier team; progress in the senior league and national Football Association was more difficult, but they and their supporters continue to thrive in their own stadium – back 'home' in St Mary's parish. (G. Chalk and D. Juson's History of Southampton Football Club, Saintsfc.co.uk)

NOVEMBER 22ND

1887: On this day Daniel Day, one of the original All England Cricketers, died, aged eighty-one.

Day had been playing cricket during the period when bowling evolved from the round-arm style to overarm bowling in the 1860s. He was acknowledged to be the outstanding professional bowler of the time, being described as 'first rate, rather fast, with a high delivery, his balls getting up quick from the ground'. One of his most memorable performances was playing for Hampshire, against the MCC at Lord's in 1842. He scored seventy runs and took ten wickets, helping Hampshire to defeat the MCC by 235 runs. Day was also a member of the All England XI team for the Players versus Gentlemen matches at Lord's. To support himself he became the licensee of a number of different public houses around the town, and was especially associated with the Antelope cricket ground, which eventually became known as Day's. On his death he requested that his batting gloves, favourite old bat and walking stick were all buried with him: symbols of his career as a great player and umpire. (Friends of Southampton Old Cemetery Newsletter, May 2008)

NOVEMBER 23RD

1784: On this day, John Kunnison was declared bankrupt at a hearing in the Star Hotel in the High Street. There had been two other humiliating days before this final hearing, when arrangements were made for the assessment of his belongings, and the amounts payable to his various creditors were agreed upon.

Like several other traders, Kunnison had overstretched himself attempting to exploit the many visitors to the eighteenth-century town. Southampton was a thriving spa and health resort at this time, and visitors came from many parts of the country, especially London. Kunnison was a well-known wine merchant and leather manufacturer, but he was tempted by the fashionable fabrics and muslins which the visiting ladies seemed eager to buy. He developed a large warehouse and shop in St Michael's Square, bringing all the latest fabrics down from London – but the establishment closed and the stock was sold off at a 15 per cent reduction 'to save the expense of returning it to London'. Sadly, London traders regularly followed the visitors from the capital, rented local shops in the High Street, and sold their goods not only to the visitors but to the locals as well. Poor Kunnison stood no chance! (*London Gazette*, 12 October 1784; *Salisbury Journal*, 12 October 1772)

NOVEMBER 24TH

1795: On this day, a public meeting was called to discuss plans for a bridge across the River Itchen.

The bridge had been needed for a long time, particularly because of the variability of the weather on the river. There were frequent complaints about the disruption caused by violent winds and tides at Itchen Ferry. (It is not clear if the report is referring to the actual ferry crossing, or the village of the same name.) Other advantages of having a bridge would include shortening the distance to Portsmouth, Gosport and Chichester, and this would improve communication between Southampton and the country lying on the eastern side of the Itchen, along the Great Western Road. Residents were encouraged to attend a public meeting on 2 December, in the Guildhall, to view the various plans for the project and further the plans for a public subscription, which would be repaid with interest earned from the tolls. (*Hampshire Chronicle*, 28 November 1795)

November 25th

1925: On this day, Herbert Collins set up the Swaythling Housing Society.

Collins was one of the leading Garden City architects. Working with Fred Woolley, a leading local figure, and Claude Ashby from Bursledon Brickworks, he set out to alleviate the shortage of affordable housing in the area. As the Society's name suggests, their first houses were built in Swaythling, with a weekly rent of 10s 6d for a three-bedroom house. Two-bedroom houses were cheaper, of course. Collins went on to design many of the suburban developments around Southampton with his own distinctive style, with groups of terraced or semi-detached houses clustered around wide greens. Several of his estates have been designated as conservation areas, and he gained national recognition for his style and work in the design of affordable housing. Many of his homes still exist and it is a point of pride for those who live in them to be able to say, 'I live in a Collins house.' (*Southern Daily Echo*, 21 June 2007; A. Rance, *Southampton: An Illustrated History*, Southampton, 1980)

NOVEMBER 26TH

1669: On this day, the town decided to order brass blanks to produce its own coinage.

The country was bankrupt and there was a shortage of legal money. John Evelyn, the diarist, had complained in 1655 that there was so much 'clipped' money that there was scarcely any worth more than half its face value. The 'coiners' clipped small amounts of metal from legal money, melted it down and mixed this with base metals to make counterfeit money. 'Coining' was a capital offence, but few were arrested because many people believed that there would be no money at all without their efforts, and they also provided employment. By 1669 things were even worse and many traders were making their own 'money' in the form of tokens. Like other town authorities, Southampton Corporation felt they should produce a more standardised form of local currency (which was distributed on 1 January). Nationally the situation continued to deteriorate, and it was only when the government finally agreed to the Royal Mint producing a completely new coinage, in 1695, that some stability was restored. (J.C. Jeaffreson, *The Manuscripts of the Corporations of Southampton and King's Lynn*, 1887, p.31; M. Gaskill, *Crime and Mentalities in Early Modern Britain*, Cambridge, 2002, pp.123-203)

NOVEMBER 27TH

1703: On this night, from midnight until 6 a.m., the Great Storm came from the North Atlantic and struck southern England and Wales, before crossing to Scandinavia and the Baltic Ocean. Its ferocity and 70mph winds cut a 300-mile wide swathe of devastation across the countryside. Eight thousand people were killed on land and one fifth of the navy was lost, together with unknown numbers of merchant seamen and vessels.

So how did Southampton fare? No buildings escaped damage, many chimneys were blown down, roofs lost part or all of their tiles, and numerous great trees were blown down. Luckily there were no deaths, but the local shipping suffered. Mostly this was because the ships had been moored in the river, or at the quays, so that when the wind struck it drove them ashore. Many were totally wrecked, but others were driven inshore onto the soft mud for long distances. The owners unloaded the cargo and then dug long channels, in the hope that the high tides might float the vessels off. (D. Defoe, *The Storm*, R. Hamblyn (ed.), London, 2003, p.130)

November 28th

1900: On this day, the Parliamentary Debating Society debated the question of female suffrage.

The chief arguments against the motion included the viewpoint that women, on the whole, did not want the vote, and they were too sentimental and emotional to be trusted with the control or participation in state affairs should they be elected to Parliament. Imagine the situation of husband, wife and daughter all in Parliament: 'what a rough time poor Pa would have after a debate'. Supporters of the motion spoke of the good work already achieved by women in public positions, and the benefits felt in countries where they already had the franchise. Granting the vote to women was progress and only a matter of time. The motion won by five votes. (*Southern Daily Echo*, 28 November 1900)

———◆———

1900: On this day, the Tanners Brook bus in Southampton was withdrawn when it was found that none of the twelve horses used to draw the vehicle were in a fit state to work. (*Southampton and the Region 1900-1999: Echoes of a Century*, Daily Echo)

November 29th

1777: On this day, Thomas Harder of the Bell Savage Inn at Ludgate Hill proudly announced that he had repaired and renovated the establishment in the most elegant manner.

It had accommodation for gentlemen or families from the country, had a large room for the entertainment of companies, and could supply dinners at the shortest notice. Coaches and waggons set out for the establishment each day from Southampton. This was only one of several coaching businesses that linked Southampton to London, underlining the importance of the port for business, international travel and the tourist trade. (*Gazetteer & New Daily Advertiser*)

———•◆•———

1834: On this day, a notice was published to inform mariners that an oil lamp would be fixed and lit at Calshot Castle during the winter months.

NOVEMBER 30TH

1940: On this day the town suffered one of its worst air raids. This graphic account was written by the rector of Millbrook Church, as he and his family spent the night in their air-raid shelter.

> As I write a terrific air battle is going on above us – sirens 6.15 and immediately planes and gunfire – a heavy attack on So'ton at once developed – terrific explosions all around us – shrapnel like rain – a series of explosions for minutes close by – bombs are falling all around shaking our shelter to the foundations – God be merciful to all ... bombs have again fallen near, shaking the shelter like a ship's cabin in a rough sea – 7.21 a stray shell – 7.22 bombs – 7.23 guns start again and 7.31 planes over again – 7.37 seven severe explosions shook us – a plane dives nearby – 7.39 2 explosions – 7.46 lull – 7.51 planes again – 8.0 a lull – 8.8 zooms and guns – 8.17 crackles, like stones on stones ... large fires visible – 8.22 nearer zooms – 8.29 very heavy fire – 8.44 zooms and guns – 8.46 whistler bombs – 8.49 peeped out – the sky all red over the town – 8.55 whistles and bombs – 8.54 many planes over. ...

What the rector describes are the divebombers ('zooms'), the whistler bombs, and broken electricity cables lashing around in the air ('crackles, like stones on stones'). (Revd J.L. Beaumont James' Diary: private collection)

DECEMBER 1st

1860: On this day the *La Plata* caught fire at 1 a.m. The big wooden ship was 4ft thick overall and 6ft thick at the bows.

It had been moored alongside the coaling jetty overnight. Smoke was noticed by the tide surveyors, who raised the alarm and rang the docks' firebell. A message was sent to Bargate police station – but neither the bell there nor the one at the Audit House was rung, nor was a message sent to the Ordnance Survey Office to bring the Royal Engineers. Southampton fire brigade arrived promptly, but the suction pipe was too short to reach the water (then at low tide) and the engine was not in proper working order. The firemen's efforts produced jeers and insults from those working the smaller machines of the docks and shipping lines. The town engine was useless. Since the town bells had not been rung, there was a shortage of manpower. Royal Engineers finally arrived after 5 a.m. and got to work. The docks' bell was rung again and, shortly afterwards, hundreds of willing hands arrived to man the engines. Eventually there were eleven jets of water pouring into the fire. It was declared to be safe by 7 a.m. (*Hampshire Advertiser*)

DECEMBER 2ND

1681: On this day Elizabeth Loder was barbarously murdered in the Porters Field, now known as Queen's Park. Her body was then buried in St Mary's churchyard, but she was not allowed to rest in peace for long. Six days later, she was 'diged up for John Norborn and others to touch her body'.

There were two popular superstitions concerning the bodies of murder victims; firstly that they could miraculously cure various sicknesses, and secondly that they would bleed if touched by the murderer, so revealing his, or her, identity. The account given in the parish register of All Saints' Church gives no clue which was intended on this occasion. Were these people hoping for a cure, or were they all suspected of her murder and obliged to touch her to prove their innocence or guilt? (All Saints' Church burial registers)

DECEMBER 3RD

1763: On this day, bees owned by John Allen at Bishopstoke were 'gathering wax as if it was midsummer'. (*Lloyds Evening Post*)

---•◆•---

1938: On this day, the *Normandie* was delayed by a docks strike in France. Passengers hoping to embark had all been contacted, by telephone or telegram, to inform them of the delay. They would be embarking from Southampton, when the liner arrived at her berth on the Mother Bank at Ryde on the Isle of Wight. Tenders would be taking passengers, baggage and mail from Southampton to the liner. (*Southern Daily Echo*)

---•◆•---

1979: On this day Prince Charles, the Prince of Wales, attended a memorial tribute to his uncle, Lord Louis Mountbatten, killed earlier that year in Ireland. The tribute was held in Southampton's Guildhall and was attended by many local people. The Mountbattens' family home, Broadlands, was only a few miles away. It was said that Lord Louis had 'packed more excitement and adventure into his seventy-nine years than any human being had a right to expect'. (*Southern Daily Echo*)

DECEMBER 4TH

1847: On this day, a deputation of fifty tradesmen from the town complained to the Improvement Committee of the council.

They each kept a few pigs within the town, and had been served with notices to remove the animals within four days. 'Many indulged in no very polite expressions with reference to the gentlemen of the Improvement Board.' The Improvement Act said that anyone keeping a pig or pigsty had to remove it if a complaint was made. The deputation asked who had complained, since there was no longer a street-keeper, and the Chairman explained that the job had been taken over by the police. A pamphlet had been distributed to explain the situation – it had become known as Whigs versus Pigs (the Whigs being the ruling political party). The police had been told to look for the manure heaps first, but instead they had seen the pigs and ignored the manure heaps. A councillor complained that the amount of manure and mud in the town was bad. He had recently stepped backwards off the kerb to allow a lady to pass and found himself ankle-deep in a pile of the mixture! (*Hampshire Advertiser & Salisbury Guardian*)

DECEMBER 5TH

1830: On this day, Frederick Bridell was baptised at St Mary's Church. He would become a landscape painter often compared with Turner, especially in his treatment of sea, sky, cloud and mist.

Born at Houndwell Place, Southampton, Bridell 'drew avidly' from the age of nine, but his father wanted him to become a builder. As a compromise, Frederick became a house painter while continuing with his own art. In 1848 he took a five-year contract to travel Britain copying the work of great artists. This was the only art education he ever received, and, when the contract was extended to include Europe, he was able to perfect his technique. At the same time, he produced his own landscape paintings, developing a simple style completely at variance with the Pre-Raphaelite fashions of the era. Eventually, in the late 1850s, he began to receive recognition, and his pictures were exhibited at Liverpool, Manchester and the Royal Academy. Living in Southampton, Bridell was commissioned to do work for J.H. Wolff, the shipping magnate, who assembled a collection in his home, Bevois Mount House, forming the Bridell Gallery. The artist died from tuberculosis in 1863, and in 1864 the collection was passed to Southampton Art Gallery. (Dictionary of National Biography online)

DECEMBER 6TH

1802: On this day, a local wager was reported which was obviously considered foolhardy.

A gardener by the name of Penny had gambled 7 guineas that he could ride to Romsey and back within two hours. The starting point was agreed to be the Pound Tree, Above Bar. This was the tree where loose horses and/or carts were tied up until claimed and paid for by their owners. The history of parking offences goes back a long way in Southampton. At 7 a.m., Mr Penny set out, and reached the Romsey turnpike road within the hour. The road was very muddy and heavy, 'and the man being nearly sixty years of age, his friends persuaded him to give it up'. The distance was upwards of 14 miles. This story gives considerable insight into travel conditions and attitudes towards age at that time. (*Hampshire Chronicle*, 6 December 1802)

1857: On this day, Equator Maria Oneida Brown was baptised at St Michael's Church. She had been born on 29 July 1857, on the steamship *Oneida* as the ship 'crossed the line'; in other words, it had sailed across the equator. (*See* October 19th) (St Michael's parish baptism registers)

DECEMBER 7TH

1921: On this day, it was reported that a farmworker had resigned.

Perhaps not a particularly newsworthy item at first glance, but Sam (this was the only name he would give) had an unusual complaint about his work. Sam had worked on his present employer's farm for nine years, and presumably had seen many changes to both the farm and his own working conditions during that time. This was just three years after the First World War, and the influenza pandemic immediately following. There was a big campaign to improve the nation's health by improved diet, and farmers, gardeners and other individuals were being encouraged to keep hens for egg production. Sam's employer switched to poultry farming and wished to keep track of the best poultry breeds for egg production. He therefore got Sam to write on every egg, in indelible pencil, the date it was laid and the breed of hen that had produced it. This was too much and Sam resigned, with the following explanation: 'I've done every kind of rotten job on the farm for nine years, but blowed if I'd rather not starve than go on being secretary to your d****d hens!' (*Southern Daily Echo*)

DECEMBER 8TH

1952: On this day, the smog in London caused disruption in Southampton.

Three days earlier the smog, a mixture of fog and smoke, had descended on London. Without any wind to blow it away, and exacerbated by near-freezing temperatures which increased the number of coal fires being lit, the smog remained in the city, bringing everything to a halt. The first casualties were cattle at the Smithfield Agricultural Show. Despite being provided with respirators, six animals died from the smog, including a prize-winning heifer owned by a West Tisted farmer. At Sadler's Wells, an opera had to be stopped because there was so much smog in the theatre. Schools closed because it was too dangerous to go out, cars were abandoned, and buses, trains and planes were stopped as visibility was so bad. In Southampton a similar picture was emerging, but here the smog did not linger so long – the breezes from the coast did clear it occasionally, although it returned each morning as the household fires were lit. Hurn Airport, near Bournemouth, received fifty planes diverted from London. It reported having dealt with 1,000 passengers in four days! (*Southern Daily Echo*, reports from 5 December through to 8 December 1952)

DECEMBER 9TH

1808: On this day, Jane Austen recorded that she had attended a ball at the Dolphin, in Southampton, where she had also danced fifteen years before. She wrote that, 'inspite of the shame of being so much older, [I] felt with thankfulness that I was quite as happy now as then'.

The evening had started when they were called for at just gone 9 p.m., and they had returned just before midnight. The ball was 'tolerably full and there were perhaps thirty couple of dancers – the melancholy part was to see so many dozen young women standing by without partners, and each of them with two ugly naked shoulders!' She records that there were only four dances during the evening, and she was obviously pleased to have been asked to dance with a foreign gentleman of nodding acquaintance, who had fine black eyes. The Austens lived in a house in Castle Square between 1807 and 1809, after spending the previous year lodging in the town. Altogether, Jane spent three years in the port and appears to have enjoyed her time there. (D. Le Faye, *Jane Austen's Letters,* Letter 62, Oxford, 1997)

DECEMBER 10TH

2007: On this day the *Queen Victoria* liner was named by the Duchess of Cornwall.

The naming of the new Cunarder had prompted five days of events in the town, culminating in the naming ceremony itself, performed by the Duchess, accompanied by the Prince of Wales. Guests were treated to a display of fireworks and water fountains as an accompaniment to Bizet's music from *Carmen*, prior to the traditional bottle of champagne being smashed on the ship's bows. Lavishly fitted out using marble, wood and plush soft furnishings, the 90,000-ton liner was destined to undertake long cruises for 2,000 passengers, who would be served by 1,001 crew members. A floating town and hotel combined, the ship aims to provide for the passengers' every need. It does seem just a little unfortunate, however, that the new liner's facilities are described as 'luxurious White Star Service'. (Various online *Queen Victoria* liner sites)

DECEMBER 11TH

1607: On this day the town musicians, William Greene and William Tompson, received their new livery.

They collected five black broadcloth (hardwearing woollen material) coats, because five was the usual number of musicians expected to play for events. In addition, as town officials, Greene and Tompson received silver badges of office to wear. However, they were expected to indemnify the Corporation for the value of the badges, which weighed 4oz each and cost 40s. These two were the permanent town musicians; others were co-opted into the band as and when needed and, if they were of sufficiently good standard, they could join them. Two months later, a complaint was brought against Tompson for having a stranger living in his house. Moreover, it was a girl who had just given birth. The officials were assured that neither girl nor child would cost the town any money. A year later Tompson was harbouring a different woman, who was a stranger to the town, so she was ordered to leave. Morality was only an issue if money was at stake! (J. Horrocks, *Assembly Books of Southampton, Vol. I, 1602-1608*, Southampton, 1917, pp.43, 50)

DECEMBER 12TH

1873: On this day Tommy Lewis, son of a Jersey dock worker, was born in St Mary's parish, Southampton.

He started work as a watchmaker in the town, aged eleven, and by his mid-teens was already involved with the Labour movement. In 1901, not yet thirty, he was elected as Southampton's first Labour councillor and served almost continuously until 1961. He became one of the town's first two Labour MPs in 1929. However, it was his role in the development of local trade unionism where he exerted the most influence. Sometimes controversial, his concerns nonetheless were always in defence of the workers. Lewis went to Plymouth with other members of the British Seafarers' Union, in 1912, to speak to the rescued crewmembers of the *Titanic*, who were held there pending the British Inquiry. Finding themselves banned from entering the docks, the Union officials hired a small boat and addressed the crew from the water. As well as founding the British Seafarers' Union in 1911, Lewis was responsible for extending the influence of a variety of other unions in the town. The Swaythling Link, A335 bypass, is named Thomas Lewis Way to commemorate this champion of ordinary people. (F. Craig, *British Parliamentary Election Results 1918-1949*, 1983)

DECEMBER 13TH

1921: On this day, the *Southern Daily Echo* reported on a new labour-saving device, following a demonstration of its use.

The apparatus consisted of an alarm clock, a kettle and an electric lamp. The clock was set in the usual way and, when the alarm went off, the mechanism switched on and lit the gas ring under the kettle. When the water in the kettle boiled the gas was turned off, the light turned on and a bell was rung. The inventor claimed to have been using the invention for over twenty years. The whole thing sounds very familiar nowadays: an automatic tea or coffee maker. What does make the report remarkable is the use of a gas ring, together with a means of turning the gas on and off as well as lighting it. This was in an age of coal gas, which was highly toxic when breathed in, and very explosive. How ever the invention is viewed, its inventor was very lucky to have survived its use for twenty years. The report remarked that the age of automatic domestic service appeared to have come nearer. (*Southern Daily Echo*)

DECEMBER 14TH

1608: On this day, the barbers agreed not to trim on the Sabbath.

This was a longstanding agreement dating from a previous mayoralty, and it had been infringed by one of their number, who had paid 2s 6d to the poor in recompense. The new agreement gave exceptions for 'gentlemen strangers who should be in the town, or who should resort to it and desire to be trimmed at such otherwise forbidden time'. Perhaps this was intended to ensure that strangers were tidy enough to attend church. Thirty years later, coincidentally on the same date, Martin Peale (a barber-surgeon) was in trouble for insolent behaviour and unmannerly language towards the Assembly. He seems to have been annoyed because he had been appointed by the Bishop, but had not been entered by the town authorities as a freeman to follow his trade. The Assembly condemned him because such 'proud and peremptory language of so mean a fellow in this place is not to be endured'. They then demanded that he appear at the next court sessions to explain himself. Sadly, the outcome is not known. (J.S. Davies, *A History of Southampton*, Southampton, 1883, p.266)

DECEMBER 15TH

1584: On this day the Spanish ambassador, M. de Segur, complained about the number of pirates in the Southampton area.

He certainly describes a desperate situation. He was hoping to embark for his return home, but was obliged to wait for some time in the town, until an armed escort of vessels could be provided to see him safely into the Channel. De Segur's complaints were made in a letter to Francis Walsingham, Queen Elizabeth's spymaster. In it, he says that he could not have chosen a worse place to embark; pirates guarded the mouth of the river and, only the day before, a Jersey vessel had been attacked and prevented from entering the port, and the pirates regularly came right up to the quays and walls of the town. The entire Solent was swarming with them and their activities extended as far as Poole. Naval vessels kept them away from Portsmouth, but this only made matters worse for other ports along the coast. The Spaniard rightly painted an alarming picture of the situation, but he was possibly unaware that some of these 'pirates' were likely to have been privateers, working on behalf of the Queen, as did both Sir Francis Drake and Sir Walter Raleigh. (J.S. Davies, *A History of Southampton*, Southampton, 1883, p.481)

DECEMBER 16TH

1912: On this day, Southampton's newest motor fire engine, considered to be the last word in firefighting, was christened in compliment to the Mayoress.

The ceremony took place at the Corporation baths, attended by Mayor Bowyer, the Mayoress and their two children. Mrs Bowyer performed the christening ceremony by breaking a bottle of wine across the bonnet of the fire engine, and the Union Jack, draped across the front, was removed to reveal a brass plate with the name 'Madeline' engraved on it. Mrs Bowyer was invited to climb into the driving seat, and she then started the engine up for a demonstration of the machine's powers. Drawing water from the baths, the fire engine produced three powerful jets of water, each attaining a height of 100ft; when two of these were shut down, a single jet of water reaching approximately 220ft was produced. The machine was considered to be an important addition to the safety of the town. (*Southern Echo*)

DECEMBER 17TH

1596: On this day John Major, the senior bailiff, was put into the debtors' prison.

He had been summoned to the Audit House in the morning to account for non-payment of various debts owing not only to the council, but twelve other town burgesses. At first he was apologetic, but when it became apparent that the officials were going to impose a fine, take away his burgess-ship, and threaten him with the debtors' prison, he flew into a rage, saying he didn't care what they did, he was going to go about his trade whether he was a burgess or not. Then he stormed out and went home. In the afternoon, the Piepowder Court was due to be held in the Guildhall, directly above the Counter Prison for debtors. As the court was convened, so John Major, wearing his full regalia as senior bailiff, arrived and attempted to take his place as a judge of the court. The Mayor told him sternly that he was neither burgess nor bailiff, and was not wanted in the court. Major flew into another rage and, still shouting and ranting, was pushed through the trap door of the Guildhall directly into the Counter Prison below. (T. James, *The Third Book of Remembrance of Southampton, 1514-1602, Vol. IV*, Southampton, 1979)

DECEMBER 18TH

1966: On this day a man was fined for wringing a chicken's neck.

Considering this was the time of year when many birds would suffer a similar fate, the report of this court case seems unaccountable. However, the man, an engineer, had been driven to distraction by his next-door neighbour's prized cockerel. The bird, a beautiful bantam rooster, crowed ferociously, continuously and with relentless regularity throughout the year, from 3 a.m. – summer and winter. Eventually, after suffering sleep deprivation for many months, the engineer climbed over his neighbour's fence and throttled the bird, in mid-song, before climbing back over the fence and returning to bed and undisturbed slumber. He paid the £4 fine happily, saying he would have paid £100 for a good night's sleep! (*Southern Daily Echo*, 19 December 1966)

DECEMBER 19TH

1544: On this day the town's stews (brothels) in East Street were to be closed.

The stews had been part of town life for over sixty years and probably longer. They were a useful source of income to the town because the women were regularly fined, as were married men and/or strangers who were found using their services. The brothels were run as a business, with a Master of the Stews keeping account of everything. Unfortunately, the stews were often the centre of disturbances; earlier in this year, John Lovett had been fined for 'beating the wenches', and the present master, Tristram Harrison, had been fined 'for a bloodshed' the previous year. Now, he was banned from conducting any business for and with any of the women, who were to be banished out of the town. (A. Merson, *The Third Book of Remembrance of Southampton, 1514-1602, Vol. II*, Southampton, 1955, pp.4-5)

DECEMBER 20TH

1958: On this day, the last of the flying boats left Southampton forever.

Imperial Airways had established a service at Southampton in 1938, in the New Docks, but now it was no longer viable. These were the original long-haul aircraft, being refuelled in mid-air from a converted bomber. Shortly after the inauguration of the first service, the Second World War intervened and the flying boats became long-range reconnaissance aircraft. Afterwards, two were refitted and put back into civilian service, and their long-haul routes established. A journey to Cairo took thirty-six hours, and Australia was just eight days away. Comfort was the keyword; facilities included a bar, library, and lounges with easy chairs and tables, where passengers relaxed and smoked. In 1953, flying boat *Aoete-arora* (Maori for 'Land of the Long White Cloud') took the young Queen Elizabeth and Prince Philip to New Zealand. However, by the mid-1950s, land-based airports began to expand, with bigger, faster aeroplanes. The days of the 'gentle giants' of the air were ending. The last three flew to Lisbon, supposedly to inaugurate a service there. They languished on the river for thirteen years and then were broken up. (A. Rance, *Sea Planes and Flying Boats of the Solent*, Southampton, 1981)

DECEMBER 21ST

1917: On this day it was announced that there would be a special ladies' football match at the Dell on Christmas Day.

The Saints would be playing away on Christmas Day, against their greatest rivals Portsmouth, and had, perhaps rather recklessly, agreed that the Dell could be used for this fixture. The *Daily Echo* reported that 'the fair players are understood to be very keen on the event and they confess it should produce plenty of fun, if nothing else'. Apparently nobody took the concept of ladies' football seriously, including the potential players. However, various ladies' teams were being formed in factories throughout the country as a morale booster to local communities. One of the most successful, Dick, Kerr & Co., based in Preston, also played its first match on Christmas Day in 1917, and continued to play as part of a ladies' league after the war; by 1921 they had abandoned long skirts for shorts. The Southampton ladies of 1917 did not maintain their interest, and it was not until 1979 that the city had its own ladies' football team. (*Southern Daily Echo*, 20 December 1917; Dick, Kerr 1917 Ladies Football online)

DECEMBER 22ND

1849: On this day there was a driving accident in the New Road.

A four-wheel trap being driven by Mr Fuller, of French Street, suffered a most unfortunate accident when the horse suddenly took fright, broke away from the trap and galloped homewards, throwing Mr Fuller out. The horse, continuing on its flight through the town, turned the corner into West Street, slipped and fell, kicking in two plate-glass windows in Mr Jolliffe's tailor's shop. Mr Fuller was taken to Mr Bond's house in Orchard Lane, where he was found to be only slightly injured and was reported to be making a good recovery at home. (*Hampshire Advertiser & Salisbury Guardian*)

DECEMBER 23RD

1944: On this day, the 14th US Major Port gave a huge Christmas party for the children of Southampton. The party took place in the Civic Centre Guildhall, with bunting and paper hats, lemonade, cake and trifle, all followed by a conjuror. For the adults present, it provided some colour and relief from the austere rationing of everyday civilian life. For many of the children it was a glimpse into a world they had never known.

During the six months since D-day, two million Americans had passed through the town, producing mixed feelings among the civilian population. British 'Tommies' disliked the Americans' popularity with the girls. The Americans' smart uniforms and apparently never-ending supply of sweets and cigarettes seemed, for many, a distant memory of lost days. It also gave rise to the famous comment that there were three things wrong with the Americans: they were 'over-paid, over-sexed and over here'. Some Americans were billeted with Southampton families and it was, no doubt, this experience which gave birth to the idea of giving the local children a Christmas party – they had been reminded of their own children left behind in the USA. Many of them would never have another Christmas with their families again. (A. Rance, *Southampton: An Illustrated History*, Southampton, 1980, p.171)

DECEMBER 24TH

1888: On this day a well-dressed woman, apparently from a respectable address, was brought before the Police Court for causing a nuisance to a local clergyman.

Claiming to be a member of his family, she constantly sent him letters of endearment, even when he had consistently returned them unopened. The woman insisted that he had replied to them through the 'agony' column in the *Standard*. After questioning, it appeared that she had been baptised by the clergyman and this had sparked off the delusion that she was a member of his family. Her delusions sometimes included other members of his family as well. Eventually she had presented herself at his house and announced she had come to stay! The cleric had called a doctor, who called the police, who said they could only charge her for being a 'wandering lunatic' and lock her up, and so she made an appearance before the court. The reverend did not want her to be locked up, and eventually the court persuaded the woman to go to the poor house. (*Southern Echo*)

DECEMBER 25TH

1752: On this day, many people from Southampton went into the New Forest to observe whether the Cadnam Oak had produced any leaves. The tree was reputed to burst into leaf on Christmas Day.

In 1752, the calendar had been changed from the Julian to the Gregorian style that we are familiar with today. In 1752, this meant that eleven days had been 'lost' and Christmas Day was brought forward; it would now be celebrated on 25 December, instead of 6 January. The people of Southampton, therefore, looked for verification of the new calendar by observing if the Cadnam Oak had produced its leaves on the new Christmas Day. When they arrived ...

> ... finding no Buds or Appearance of green Leaves, [they] came away greatly dissatisfied with the Alteration of the Day: And on Friday last, being old Christmas, they went again, and to their great Joy found the Oak blown and several Branches almost cover'd with green leaves; some of which they brought away with them. This Circumstance has served to convince Abundance that the new Christmas day is wrong, and they are henceforth determined to keep only the old.

(Report from Southampton, 12 January 1753, printed in *Salisbury Journal*, 15 January 1753)

DECEMBER 26TH

1912: On this day, Millbank Street and the surrounding Northam streets were flooded to a depth of 3ft.

The proximity of the river meant that this low-lying area of the town had always been at risk of flooding, and it occurred almost annually; dead rats came out of the sewers and mud was deposited everywhere. Families retreated to live upstairs in their houses until the water subsided. Transport was difficult; those with small rowing boats were better off, but even the tin baths most people had were pressed into service. Children were unable to get to school – partly due to lack of transport, but also for fear of the water. Some remembered that when they returned to school they were asked if they had lost their shoes in the water; if they had, they were given a new pair of wooden clogs. The Mayor's Fund also provided each home that had suffered flooding with hundredweight of coal, to provide the family with at least some warmth to start the drying-out process – after all, it was Christmas. (S. Jemima, *Chapel and Northam*, Southampton City Council)

DECEMBER 27TH

1879: On this day, the artist William Shayer was buried at St James' Church, Shirley.

He had been one of the most prolific artists in the area, refusing to live in London, closer to the Royal Academy, because his inspiration came from the Hampshire countryside, especially the New Forest. Gypsies figured in many of his paintings, probably as a result of his friendship with James Crabb (*see* April 13th). Many paintings included a grey pony – the Shayer family pet. Shayer had trained originally as a coach painter, painting the owners' Coats of Arms on the coaches. When he lived in French Street, he also painted scenery for the theatre there, as well as inn signs and funerary hatchments; the one he did for Admiral Charles Bullen can be found in St James' Church. Having married twice, this almost frenetic production was his only means of supporting his large family of ten children. Sadly, in 1870, his sight began to fail and he had to give up painting, spending the last of his ninety-two years in total darkness. (Friends of Southampton Old Cemetery Newsletter, January 2008; St James' Shirley parish registers)

DECEMBER 28TH

1500: On this day the burgesses, led by the Mayor, broke down the hedges enclosing the Saltmarsh.

This was a dispute over the common rights traditionally held for the Saltmarsh, located between God's House tower and the River Itchen. Common rights had been claimed over the Saltmarsh from at least 1228. Unfortunately, the master of God's House also made a claim to it, and enclosed the land with hedges and ditches to prevent the townspeople using it for pasture. Thus the stage was set for a showdown. So a small army of burgesses, led by the Mayor and armed with sticks, shovels and machetes, moved onto the Saltmarsh, hacked the master's hedges and fences down, and filled in the ditches. The master of God's House referred the dispute to the King and council. The Corporation brought forward various ancient residents to testify that the town had had common rights on the Saltmarsh since 'time out of mind'. They won their case and the Saltmarsh remained common land. (C. Platt, *Medieval Southampton*, 1973, pp.50-1; J.S. Davies, *A History of Southampton*, Southampton, 1883, pp.52-4)

DECEMBER 29TH

1903: On this day, a report was made about Christmas Day in Southampton Workhouse. The Board of Guardians, their wives and friends, had shared in the celebrations with the workhouse inmates.

The Guardians had the building decorated (this was most tastefully done, according to the report) with golden chrysanthemums worked into trelliswork, proclaiming a message to the official visitors: 'Happiness and all Good Luck be with you.' The inmates had made a banner for the Guardians, wishing them a happy Christmas, and the hall and staircase were brightly decorated. Unfortunately, the boys were in quarantine (no explanation is given), so that the number of residents attending appeared fewer than in previous years. After dinner, gifts were distributed to the inmates; the men received tobacco, the women were given the choice of snuff or tea, and the children were all given oranges, sweets and nuts. In the evening they were entertained with a magic lantern show, followed by a sing-song. (*Southern Daily Echo*, 29 December 1903)

DECEMBER 30TH

1320: On this day, the licence to rebuild Holy Rood Church was granted.

The church was in need of repair and enlargement, but more importantly it needed to be moved back a few yards. Its existing situation was inconvenient because it obstructed the High Street (English Street, as it was then) and was therefore an impediment to traffic and trade. Notwithstanding the difficulties of dismantling and rebuilding the church, there were the legalities associated with buying the bigger, more easterly plot of land that was needed. Eventually negotiations were completed and the new plot, 140ft long by 120ft wide, was acquired, and the agreement to start building the new church was arranged. With the help of various leading parishioners (no doubt eager to have their own church again), the new church was completed within the next thirteen years, about 20ft east of its original position, where it still stands today. (C. Platt, *Medieval Southampton*, 1973, pp.96-8)

DECEMBER 31ST

1517: On this day, Widow Cowart received a letter from King Henry VIII.

Whilst visiting Southampton, the King wrote to the widow of Nicholas Cowart, a past Mayor of the town, and recommended that she take William Symonds as her second husband. William was one of the sewers of the King's chamber and the King apparently pleaded his case most vigorously, even including a personal token from himself. Sir John Dawtrey, from Tudor House, had also spoken to the widow, pleading William Symonds' case. Faced with such an onslaught, how could she not accept William's proposal? After all, the King was used to getting his own way when dealing with women. (J.S. Davies, *A History of Southampton*, Southampton, 1883, p.477; King Henry VIII's letters online)

———•◆•———

1949: On this day the last tram made its final ceremonial journey from the floating bridge to the Shirley depot, arriving just before the New Year heralded in the second half of the twentieth century. (A. Rance, *Southampton: An Illustrated History*, Southampton, 1980, p.177)